W9-ADW-862

A PRIDE OF
BENTLEYS

A PRIDE OF
BENTLEYS

BY JOHN ADAMS & RAY ROBERTS

CHARTWELL
BOOKS INC.

Copy Editors: Nicola Davies
William J. Howell
Art Editor: Deborah Miles
Design: Mark Holt

Published by Chartwel Books Inc.
A Division of Book Sales Inc.
110 Enterprise Avenue
Secaucus, New Jersey 07094

First published in 1978 by New English Library
Limited, Barnard's Inn, Holborn, London EC1N 2JR, England

© Text and illustrations copyright Colourviews Limited 1978.

Set in 10/11 point Plantin by South Bucks Typesetters Limited.
Printed and bound by Fratelli Spada, Ciampino, Rome, Italy

ISBN - O - 89009 - 228 - I

All rights reserved. Except for use in reviews, no part of this book
may be reproduced, in any form or by any means, without the
prior written permission of the publishers

Page 2:
**Painting by Frank Wootton: by courtesy of 'Harpers &
Queen'.**

Contents

Introduction

From the delivery of the first production model in September 1921 up to the present day, the name Bentley has been regarded with awe by schoolboys and with reverence and devotion by those who are older. The Bentley has always been a car to create excitement in the beholder and unbounded enthusiasm from the owner, so much so that the Bentley Drivers Club is one of the oldest single-make car clubs in the World. For those old enough to remember, the sight of a 4½-litre or a Speed Six high on the railway bank at Brooklands was a thrilling experience.

However, only a small proportion of the Bentleys built were ever used for racing. Most of them were very fine domestic cars with a performance which would satisfy the most sporting driver or someone who needed above average speed combined with reasonable comfort. It is remarkable to think that a car built over fifty-six years ago can still be used for regular motoring and give a performance that is not put to shame by cars of today. As the reader will soon discover, the history of the Bentley has been by no means smooth and has survived four liquidations.

There are many who think that the marque came to an end with the take-over of the original company by Rolls-Royce and do not consider the Derby and Crewe built cars as real Bentleys. Nevertheless, they are very fine motor cars and still proudly carry the winged 'B' emblem on the radiator. They were one of the fastest production cars available in the mid 1930s and later in the early 1950s the R-Type Continental was acclaimed as the fastest quality car available and a car of which to be very proud. So this is our theme — A Pride of Bentleys.

JHLA RVR

Foreword

If one accepts the definition of a cult as 'a great, often excessive, admiration of a person or idea', then certainly there is a Bentley cult, for it is doubtful if any one man and his cars have evoked such universal acclaim as W.O. Bentley.

Devotees of the marque transcend all barriers of race, creed, wealth, social status, occupation and age. Inspired by the feats of the Bentleys at Le Mans in the late 20s, those who would now be called the 'jet set' flocked to buy these great green sports-cars and the sheer majesty of the town carriages on the bigger chassis earned them a high place among the luxury cars of the world. Small wonder, then, that a few enthusiastic owners of these sporting cars banded together after a race meeting at Brooklands in 1936 to form a club for like-minded drivers. Thus the Bentley Drivers Club was born and, apart from a spell in cold storage during the Second World War, it has thrived and grown ever since.

Originally the Club was directed towards the 'Vintage' Bentleys built by 'W.O.' before the company collapsed in 1931. Their successor bearing the Bentley name had been introduced by Rolls-Royce in 1933 and was in current production at the time. These 'Silent Sports Cars' were built at the Derby factory until the outbreak of war when car production in the UK ceased for the duration of hostilities.

During the war some back-room boys at Derby had the foresight to realise that the coachbuilding capacity previously relied upon to clothe Rolls-Royce and Bentley chassis would no longer exist after the war and that a mass-produced body shell was imperative to the resumption of motor-car production. The result was that the Bentley appeared again in 1946 in the guise of the Mk VI Standard Steel Saloon. Those who labour the self-evident truth that the Bentley of today is a Rolls-Royce in all but name, would do well to remember that but for the breakaway from the 'chassis only' policy of pre-war days manifested in the Bentley Mk VI it is extremely unlikely that Rolls-Royce cars would ever have been made again.

When the Bentley Drivers Club was reactivated after the war, it was decided that the Club should embrace Bentleys built at Derby and, with the advent of the Mk VI, owners of post-war Bentleys to whom the name Bentley meant something more than just luxury high-speed transportation would be welcomed as members.

Cult, I suppose, relates to the Vintage Bentley – 'following' might be a more appropriate description of the admirers of their younger brethren. The cult of the Vintage Bentley strikes a chord in the breast of all discerning motorists–nowhere more so than among the owners of 'Derby' and 'Crewe' Bentleys, many of whom owned earlier marks in their hey-day, and many of whom have acquired them since.

Except in the eyes of a small minority of dyed-in-the-wool 'Vintagents', the admixture of all three types of Bentleys and their owners has served to make the Bentley Drivers Club one of the most highly regarded in the world. Membership is an immediate open sesame to the homes and lives of fellow-enthusiasts and it has been my good fortune to meet club members in many countries. Their dedication to the marque is unrivalled; their detailed historical and technical knowledge and their resourcefulness in maintaining and restoring their Bentleys far from the sources at hand to UK members never cease to amaze me.

I commend to you this product of three years' dogged, painstaking work by the co-authors.

When circumstances keep the hands of the Bentley driver from their customary place on the steering wheel, they will find a rewarding alternative in handling this man-size book. Once having swallowed hard and paid the price – considerably less inflated proportionately over the years than the objects of our reverence – this tome will become a prized possession fulfilling the dual role of providing hours of pleasurable gloating and a valuable reference work.

Stanley Sedgwick

Right: W.O. Bentley in thoughtful mood.

6

W. O. Bentley

Walter Owen Bentley, referred to affectionately as 'W.O.', was born on the 16 September 1888, the youngest member of a family of nine children living at Avenue Road, Regent's Park, London. He had an early interest in the steam railway engine, and he was certainly influenced by the passage of the impressive Scots Express, which he used to watch from the nearby railway bridge spanning the London and North Western Railway at what is now South Hampstead Station.

In 1905, at the age of sixteen, he went to the Great Northern Railway works at Doncaster as a premium apprentice, to train as a railway engineer. Away from the railway workshop, cricket was his first love and he spent much of his spare time at Lord's cricket ground. After he completed his apprenticeship he thought that the railway locomotive offered only a restricted future for his personal ambitions, and he soon found an outlet in motor-cycling. Two of the machines he used were a Rex and an Indian. He gained numerous gold medals in trials around 1908, raced at Brooklands and in the Isle of Man and later took to four wheels.

In 1912, with his brother H.M. Bentley, he acquired the French DFP (Deroit Flandrin et Parant) car agency, which he successfully handled until 1914 from premises in Hanover Court, London. His training as an engineer and the knowledge gained by experimenting with the aluminium pistons which were fitted to the DFP were instrumental in putting him into the uniform of a lieutenant in the Royal Naval Air Service in 1915. He was soon involved in developing the existing rotary engines for aircraft, and subsequently designed the nine-cylinder BR 1 and BR 2 engines, which were among the most successful aero engines used by Britain's First World War fighters. The BR 2 has been described as the 'ultimate in Rotary engine development', in terms of those used by the Air Force in France. It was the only true all-British radial engine to be used in the war.

After the end of the war, selling DFPs seemed a limited field for so talented an engineer, and W.O. Bentley formed his own company to design and build motor cars. He was joined by two men who helped share the design work, F.T. Burgess and H. Varley, and in October 1919, the first 3-litre Bentley engine burst into life in the small workshop in New Street Mews, off Baker Street, London.

The Bentley chassis was first shown to the public at the 1919 Motor Show, albeit with a dummy crankcase and camshaft cover on the four-cylinder 3-litre engine. The prototype had dry sump lubrication, single magneto and a Claudel Hobson carburettor. Some of the essential features of the engine were its long stroke – the con rods were 11½in (292mm) between centres – gear driven, single overhead camshaft actuating four valves per cylinder, and a deep sump, all of which produced an impressive engine nearly 3ft

(.9144m) tall; most of the main points in this basic design were to stay with successive models right up to 1930. The original 9ft 9½in 3-litre offered 1cc of engine capacity for 1lb of weight driven. Design work continued throughout the whole of 1920 in a top floor office at Conduit Street, and a very small factory was built at Oxgate Lane, Cricklewood, where development work went on apace and with such success that the first 3-litre Cricklewood car – possibly one of the experimental cars – was sold in September 1921, when a Mr Noel Van Raalte took delivery of the first production model from the Cricklewood works. It was important that this first customer should be sympathetic towards the car, as well as appreciative of its outstanding qualities. Mr Van Raalte certainly had experience, some of it gained in a slightly dubious manner while he was an undergraduate – racing a Grand Prix Mercedes in reverse gear around the streets of Cambridge!

Each Bentley produced carried a winged 'B' badge on the radiator shell, and it is generally believed that Gordon Crosby, well known for his splendid paintings of the motor car, designed this for 'W.O.' Models were normally assigned different background colours for the 'B' in the badge, these being blue, red, green and black with a white 'B', and the cars were often referred to by the non-buying public and customers as Blue Label, Red Label, etc. From time to time other colours were used but these were only to special order.

The 3-litre was an immediate success and sales increased rapidly from the small showrooms at 3 Hanover Court, just across the way from the original DFP showrooms. From 1921 to 1929 the car was produced continuously in various chassis lengths and specifications, the longest run of any model built up to 1931. The introduction in 1925 of the 3-litre speed model brought in a car immediately identified by a stoneguard which was an integral part of the radiator. Thereafter, many modifications were incorporated annually. Hard lessons learnt on rough roads and on the racing circuits led 'W.O.' to devise a front spring stop, incorporated in the front spring rear hanger bracket. Any failure of the main leaf would mean that the axle could move back about half an inch, but the car would still be able to be driven on to a garage for repairs, or even to complete a journey.

It is interesting to record that a unique 'travelling mechanic' service was provided to all owners, and cars were repaired and serviced at the customer's premises by a team of service engineers. However, by 1927/8, some seven authorised agents had been appointed between London and Glasgow who were also able to service the cars.

Bentley Motors manufactured only chassis, and the customer or dealer had bodies specially built and fitted to them. From experience gained, the company eventually designed suitable standard bodies which were built to the company's order and specifications, so that a complete car could be supplied. Vanden Plas provided no less than 380 bodies. Demand from customers on the many coachbuilders who were engaged in the business, for bigger and better bodies, which, as they grew in size increased in weight, resulted in a 'non-standard' body which often had an adverse effect on the performance of the car, due to the weight penalty it imposed. When the need for a more powerful engine to pull the heavy saloon coachwork became apparent, 'W.O.' developed a 6½-litre six-cylinder engine which was mounted in a much larger chassis. After extensive testing on the Continent it was introduced in 1925 and continued in production until 1930. Again, an engine with a very long stroke – only a little shorter than the 3-litre – was used. A variation of the standard chassis was the famous 'Speed Six', introduced in 1929.

The parade of vintage Bentleys at Oulton Park to celebrate the Golden Jubilee of Bentley Motors Ltd, 1969.

In May 1926, Captain Woolf Barnato (son of the famous diamond king, Barney Barnato), injected a large amount of capital into the company. New London showrooms were purchased at Pollen House, 10 Cork Street, and the company was re-formed. At this time H.M. Bentley left the company and took over the Hanover Street showrooms, where he started business on his own as a car sales agent.

Despite the success of the 6½, enthusiasts were asking for a more powerful four-cylinder car, so that the development work used to launch the 6½ was utilised to produce the four-cylinder 4½-litre in 1927. Again many refinements were introduced during its life, the main ones being the plate clutch replacing the original cone type in 1929, together with a heavier gauge chassis frame and self-wrapping front brakes. It is interesting to note that 'W.O.', in his endless search for quality and endurance, was possibly one of the first designers to introduce stainless steel into his cars, in about 1929. Handbrakes, bonnet fasteners, camshaft cover nuts, gear levers, engine and water jacket plates, the adjusting brake rod and bonnet handles were all made of stainless steel.

By 1930 the economic slump was beginning to be felt, and, in a possibly unwise effort to compete with Rolls-Royce and other constructors in the large car market, the six-cylinder 8-litre was produced. It had a new and even stronger frame; the rear springs were outrigged and it was fitted with a new F-Type gearbox, which

had larger bearings so that it could cope with the extra power of the 8-litre engine. It was of split-case construction, differing in this respect from all previous gearboxes built. The slump of 1931 prompted thoughts that a more economical car should also be offered and under much pressure, and against 'W.O.'s better judgement, the 4-litre, the last model built by the original Bentley Company, was marketed in 1931, after a very short period of development. But the end was in sight and the 4-litre was to have only a limited production run. Under-powered, in terms of accepted Bentley performance, with a six-cylinder 3,915cc engine in what was virtually an 8-litre chassis of reduced length, it was intended to under-price the then current Rolls-Royce opposition by about fifty pounds.

From 1924 the factory had annually fielded a team of cars to compete in major events, but shortly after the 1930 Le Mans race Bentley Motors announced its withdrawal from racing, and all participation after this was by private entry. One event in particular must be mentioned: 'Tim' Birkin's second place in the French Grand Prix at the Pau circuit, where, driving a stripped 'Blower', competing against full-blooded racing cars, he averaged 88.50mph (142.40km/h) for the 245 mile (394.2km) race!

During the period 1929 to 1931, the success of Bentley on the track and road was at its peak, and included numerous wins at Brooklands, but the domination which it achieved in the Grand Prix d'Endurance at Le Mans linked the name for ever with that famous circuit in the Department of Sarthe, France. Bentley cars have returned to Le Mans on several occasions in the post-war years to re-live past glories, and as a reminder of their undiminished reputation.

The years 1921 to 1931 saw more than 3,000 Bentleys built, many destined to live on to perpetuate the name of W.O. Bentley. This has been in no small way due to the efforts of the Bentley Drivers' Club. It is remarkable to think that over one-third of the total number of cars completed are still on the road today, in the possession of members of the club.

In 1931 the assets of Bentley Motors Ltd were acquired by Rolls-Royce and after production of all 'W.O.'-designed cars had finished, four 3-litre and six 4½-litre chassis were assembled by Rolls-Royce between 1934 and 1935, with parts left in the old company's stores. However, they were not true to original specifications, as they were built from a mixture of parts from many models. They were nearly all fitted with fully enclosed Vanden Plas bodies. Mr E. Roland Fox in his history of Vanden Plas relates how a very close relationship grew up between them and Bentley Motors. His father, Mr Edwin Fox, leased part of the Kingsbury works to 'W.O.' for use as a Service Department, and all the Le Mans racing car bodies were built by Vanden Plas under the personal scrutiny of W.O. Bentley.

If one considers the coachbuilders of the vintage era, 1920 to 1931, it is interesting to note that Vanden Plas built nearly 700 of the bodies fitted to the Bentley chassis – although Bentley Motors' service records show only 669. Five other coachbuilders, Gurney Nutting, H.J. Mulliner, Freestone and Webb, Harrison and Park Ward constructed 1,177 between them, and no less than 113 other coachbuilders supplied bodies of one type or another to the Bentley chassis; a total of 119 in all. This number was to decrease steadily up to the end of the Second World War, by which time more than half of them had disappeared. Weymann, who issued licences to build their patented body, were building bus bodies for Metro-Cammell from 1932 on, and by 1966 had been completely absorbed by that company.

3-Litre

The 3-litre was the first model built by Bentley Motors and sales commenced in 1921, though production was not properly organised until 1922. The chassis price was £1,050 and 141 were built in the first year, all of them with a wheelbase of 9ft 9½in (2.98m). Some particularly interesting points in the specification were a cylinder block and head cast in one; four valves per cylinder, the desired combustion shape achieved by valves set at an angle and driven by an overhead camshaft, and twin magnetos feeding two plugs per cylinder. 'Hour glass' pistons were used initially, but they suffered from piston slap; while they were still used for racing, the standard cars were generally fitted with a split skirt BHB (Bentley Hewitt Burgess) piston, which overcame the problem. Drive was through a cone clutch, and a close ratio A-Type gearbox with heavy straight cut gears, to a conventional rear axle. The gearbox was mounted separately and this design principle was applied to all the cars that followed. The handbrake operated on separate shoes, giving two effective rear brake systems. The suspension employed semi-elliptic springs all round, with long ones at the rear to give a good ride on the poor roads that existed at the time.

It was company policy that all chassis were to carry a five-year guarantee, and each Bentley produced had this warranty, a true reflection of the faith that 'W.O.' had in his cars. The only exception was the one-year warranty that was given to the eighteen 100mph. super sports chassis, since these of course were built with competition in mind. Competition from the earliest days was forming an integral part of the company's policy, and Bentley entered cars in every major race in which there was a chance of winning. This ensured that the cars were thoroughly track-tested. Racing success was deemed the best form of advertising. A full team of three Bentleys was entered in the 1922 Tourist Trophy race in the Isle of Man, where it won the team prize. A single entry was also sent to America for the Indianapolis 500 mile race, finishing thirteenth at over 80mph (128.72km/h).

For 1923 an alternative 10ft 10in (3.3m) wheelbase chassis was offered, fitted with the new B-Type gearbox, which employed wider ratios. A further introduction on the 9ft 9½in (2.98m) chassis was the TT replica, using an engine with a 5.3 compression ratio, and a body built by Vanden Plas. The 1922/3 sales brochure gave the guarantee of performance as: 25mpg at 30mph (48.27km/h) (open models) – and this at a time when the 11-gallon tank (49.94 litres) could be filled for the sum of 16s 9½d (old currency) and without paying any duty to the government!

Speeds in top were:

	75mph	(10ft 10in long chassis)
	(120.6km/h	– 3.302m)
	80mph	(9ft 9½in short chassis)
	(128.72km/h	– 2.98m)
	90mph	(9ft 9½in TT Replica)
	(144.8km/h	– 2.98m)

A private owner, John Duff, who was a Bentley agent, entered his early 3-litre at Le Mans in 1923 and with Frank Clement as co-driver took fourth place, watched by a very thoughtful 'W.O.', who was obviously impressed by the success and the acclaim that it

received from the crowd at the circuit.

In mid-1923 the 3-litres had front-wheel brakes fitted to a re-designed front axle. A balance gear was fitted across the frame behind the gearbox to ensure that braking effort was equally distributed between all four brake drums. It carried three complete compensators, each with two arms, the relative movement of the arms being controlled by a whiffle tree or balance arm. Another model variation was introduced in 1924: a modified TT chassis and engine, which was fitted with twin 'Sloper' carburettors, and carrying the Red Label radiator badge. It was called the 'Speed Model'. This was much in demand, with its tight road-holding and bright performance, and its popularity continued throughout the life of the 3-litre range. In 1926 and 1927 it out-sold the standard 10ft 10in (3.3m) car. In all, 513 Speed Models were built between 1924 and 1929, when the last of this series was made.

In 1924, Bentleys were again at Le Mans but this time 'W.O.' had entered an official works team, and to everyone's delight Bentley won at 53.78mph (86.53km/h) average for the twenty-four hours.

In addition to the 9ft 9½in (2.98m) Speed Model, an even faster car, the 100mph (160.9km/h) model, was offered for sale in 1925, having only a 9ft (2.7m) wheelbase. It was known as the Super Sports and had a distinctive tapering radiator. Only eighteen were built and sold in the two years of production. The chassis for this variant only had a one-year warranty, an exception to the normal five years on other models. During 1925 the radiator of the standard car was raised by one inch (25.4mm), and was given a larger header tank which eliminated the downward slope of the bonnet line of the earlier cars. Peak production of the 3-litre was reached in 1924 and 1925, with nearly 800 chassis

of all types being made. However, by 1926, the 6½-litre was on the market and only 293 3-litre chassis were completed, most of them with a one-piece sump modification to the engine. Nevertheless, 'W.O.' had decided to enter another team in the 1926 Le Mans race – three 3-litres – but it failed, due to valve and rocker troubles, and to lack of good braking.

By 1927, it seemed likely that the demand for the 3-litre was going to be affected by the 4½-litre and the successful 6½. (Only 141 of the 3-litres were built in that year.) Despite falling sales of the 3-litre, a works team again competed at Le Mans. One 4½-litre and two 3-litres, and yet again a 3-litre triumphed, after the famous 'White House' crash had wrecked the 4½-litre and one of the other 3-litre cars. Only an epic drive by Mr S.C.H. Davis and Dr J.D. Benjafield saw the surviving 3-litre through; it won despite the serious damage that it sustained in the crash. The car was forever afterwards known as 'old No 7'. It was the last year that a 3-litre was raced by the works. However the model went out in a blaze of glory. A privately-entered car won on the other side of the world, at San Martin Autodrome, Buenos Aires. It was driven by Mr E.F. Green at a creditable 84.9mph (136.60km/h) average for the 62.5 mile race (100km).

The 1928 cars had the heavier chassis and front axle, as fitted to the recently-introduced 4½-litre, together with the strong C-Type gearbox, as well as engine modifications, such as modified rockers, but only a few cars were made. Thus came to an end the model that had formed the foundation upon which the Bentley name was built. In total 1,615 cars were sold from their introduction up to 1929, all evolved from the original three experimental cars so painstakingly created by 'W.O.' Finally in 1936 four 3-litre cars were assembled by Bentley Motors (1931) Ltd, from parts taken over from the old company. These cars are known as the 'RC' series.

Left: 3-litre tourer GO 4176, chassis No 488, engine No 665, owned by K.W. Tams.

Below: A Gordon Crosby painting from a 3-litre catalogue.

Right: A contemporary catalogue illustration.

THE OUTSTANDING FEATURES OF THE THREE LITRE BENTLEY

SPECIFICATION

3-LITRE

In production from 1921 to 1929.

Basic specification at introduction (with some later production modifications).

ENGINE

4 cylinders; firing order 1, 3, 4, 2.

Bore	3.15in (80mm)
Stroke	5.87in (149mm)
Cubic capacity	2,996cc (194.7cu in)
Compression ratio	4.3:1
Brake horsepower	70
RAC rating	15.9hp

Carburettors
Claudel-Hobson, later cars had five-jet water-jacketed Smith's carburettor.

Valves and camshaft
Four tulip-shaped valves per cylinder (two inlet and two exhaust) operated by front-driven overhead camshaft running in five phosphor bronze bearings.

Cylinder block and pistons
Non-detachable head, en bloc, cast-iron. Early cars had 'hour glass pistons', later BHB split skirt type.

Crankcase and sump
Cast aluminium alloy (L5) two-piece sump, later one-piece sump.

Crankshaft
Mounted in five white metal bearings. Early cars had shell type conrods (four bolt), later con-rods had direct metal bearings.

Lubrication
Pressure feed to main bearings, big ends and overhead gear. Splash to pistons and gudgeon pins. Sump capacity 2½ gallons (11.36 litres).

Ignition
Twin synchronised MLCG4 magnetos. Two sparking plugs per cylinder. KLG J1/K1 or Champion 16.

Dynamo
Smith's 2DA driven from rear of camshaft by spider coupling—12 volt to 2 x 6 volt batteries.

Starter
Smith's 4LSA.

Instruments
1922/3 white dials; after 1923 black dials. Smith's ammeter, clock and oil gauge. AT speedometer and revolution counter.

Cooling system
Forced pump circulation, thermostat after 1923. Capacity 4¼ gallons (19.34 litres), later (1925) 4¾ gallons (21.6 litres). Fan optional but fitted to overseas cars.

Petrol system
Autovac, 2 pints (1.14 litres) from 11 gallon (50.05 litre) rear tank with two gallon (9 litres) reserve (tap on tank).

TRANSMISSION
Gearbox
Four forward speeds and reverse with positive interlock right-hand gate change. 'A' type gearbox close ratio and 'B' type wide ratio.

Ratios: 'A' type; Reverse, 2.64:1; First, 2.64:1; Second, 1.63:1; Third, 1.33:1; Top, Direct.

'B' type; Reverse, 2.64:1; First, 3.826:1; Second, 2.073:1; Third, 1.453:1; Top, Direct.

Oil capacity of both gearboxes 6 pints (3.42 litres).

Below: The 3-litre engine with twin SU type G5 carburettors.

Right: Grand Prix d'Endurance de 24 Heures, Le Mans, 14 and 15 June 1924, won by 3-litre Bentley; a contemporary catalogue illustration by Gordon Crosby.

13

Clutch
Inverted cone, Ferodo lines, 42¼in x 1¾in (1,073mm x 44.5mm).

Propeller shaft
Open one-piece with plunging (or 'pot') joints, lubricated by grease nipple.

Rear axle and final drive
Semi-floating, spiral bevel and crown wheel giving engine to road wheel ratios in top 15/53 (3.533:1) or 13/51 (3.923:1); 13/55 (4.23:1) or 14/53 (3.785:1).

Earlier cars had two bevel pinion differential, later cars four bevel pinion.

CHASSIS
Frame
Channel-section frame chassis of 0.144in (3.5mm) gauge, later 0.156in (4mm) and 0.188in (5mm) with four pressed-steel cross-members.

Suspension
Semi-eliptical front and rear springs, underslung at rear with Wefco gaiters.

Shock Absorbers
Frictional type. Hartford single at front and Duplex at rear. 1926-28 Hartford Duplex front and rear or variations most suited to work.

Brakes
Footbrake up to September 1923 operated on rear wheels only, four-wheel brakes from then onwards with Bentley-Perrot shafts to front brakes. 16in (406.4mm) drums with internal expanding shoes and Ferodo linings. Handbrake operated separate shoes to rear wheels only. Brake compensating mechanism with single-point adjustment to take up wear.

Front axle
'H'-section 40-ton high-tensile steel.

Steering
Worm and wheel, ratio 6.75:1, later 10.3:1.

Exhaust stystem
Single-piece manifold to double silencer and long tailpipe. In 1929 aluminium fishtail.

Wheels
Rudge-Whitworth detachable wire wheels with centre locking, left-hand and right-hand locking.

Tyres
Up to 1926 820mm x 120mm beaded edge, later 5.25in x 33½in (133 x 851mm) to fit 21in (533mm) well-base rims. 1928 5.25in x 21in (133mm x 533mm). From 1926 Dunlop tyres were fitted as standard.

PRINCIPAL CHASSIS DETAILS AND DIMENSIONS
Wheelbase: 1922-25 Short Standard 9ft 9½in (2.985m). 1923 Long Standard 10ft 10in (3.302m).
Track: 4ft 8in (1.422m).
Overall length: Short 13ft 3in (4.04m); Long 14ft 4½in (4.38m).
Overall body width: 5ft 8½in (1.74m).
Turning circle: (Short chassis): Right 46ft (14.02m); Left 42ft (12.8m). (Long chassis): Right 49ft (14.94m); Left 47ft (14.33m).
Ground clearance: 7¼in (184mm).

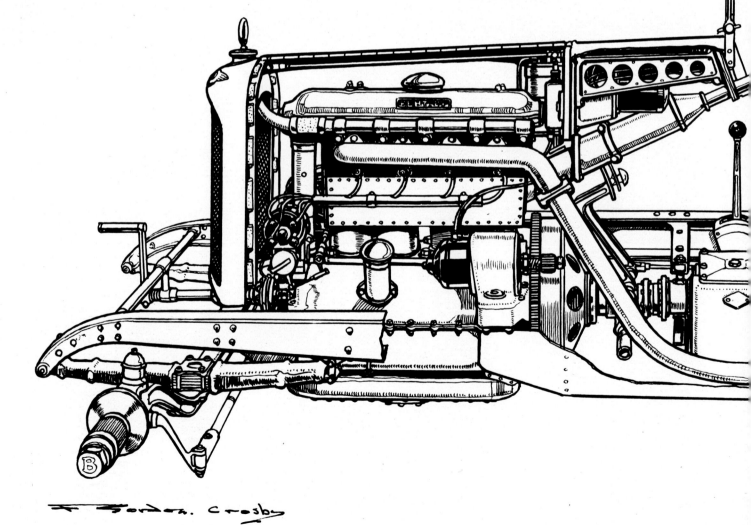

Performance:
Maximum speed: 10ft 10in Standard 75mph (120.67km/h); 9ft 9½in Standard 80mph (128.7km/h).
Petrol consumption: 18-25mpg.
Price at introduction: 1921-22 9ft 9½in chassis only £1,050.
1923 10ft 10in chassis only £1,100.
Complete car, open tourer (10ft 10in) £1,425; saloon or coupé (10ft 10in) £1,520.
Number built: 1,619 (including speed model).
Radiator badge: Blue enamel (blue label).

SPECIFICATION

3-LITRE SPEED MODEL

In production from 1923 to 1929.

Basic specification as for 3-litre except for the following variations:

ENGINE

Compression ratio	5.3:1 pre 1926	5.6:1 after 1926
Super sports	5.6:1 pre 1926	6.1:1 after 1926
Brake horsepower	80 (5.3)	85 (5.6)

Super sports had 'hour-glass' pistons.

Carburettors:

Twin SU type G5 on common induction manifold, early cars had Claudel Hobson.

TRANSMISSION
Gearbox

Early model had 'A' type box later the 'C' type:
Ratios: 'C' type; Reverse, 3.364:1; First, 3.364:1; Second, 1.823:1; Third, 1.357:1; Top, Direct.

Rear axle
14/53 (3.785:1), 13/51 (3.923:1).

CHASSIS
Steering
Ratio 10.3:1.

Exhaust
Single silencer and later special double silencer with fishtail on tail-pipe.

PRINCIPAL CHASSIS DETAILS AND DIMENSIONS
Wheelbase: 9ft 9½in (2.85m), Super Sports 9ft (2.74m).
Overall length: 13ft 3in (4.04m).
Turning circle: Right 43ft (13.11m); Left 38ft (11.58m).
Weight: Chassis 23cwt (1,159.2kg).
Open body 26-28½cwt (1,310.4-1,436.4kg).
Performance: 9ft 9½in (2.99m) 80mph (128.7km/h).
Super sports 100mph (160.9km/h).
Numbers built: Speed model (9ft 9½in) 513 ⎫ This figure is
Super sports 18 ⎬ 531. included in
⎭ 1,619 3 litres.
Chassis prices (at introduction):
Speed model £1,150 (reduced to £925 in 1924).
Complete car with open touring body £1,295 (reduced to £1,125 in 1924).
Radiator badge: 9ft 9½in red enamel (red label); Super sports green enamel (green label).

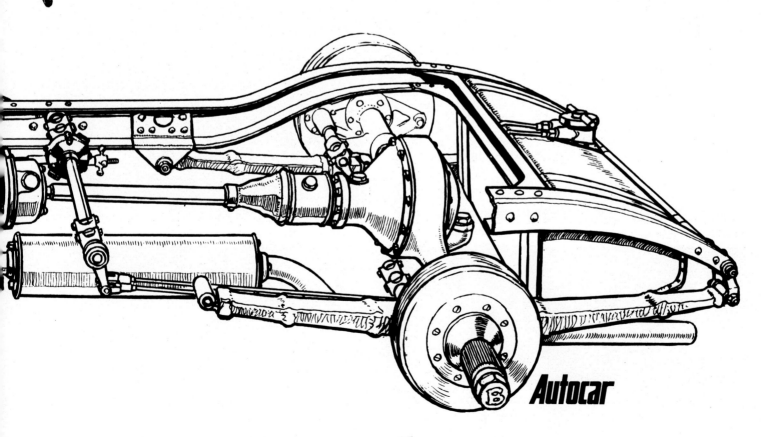

3-Litre MD9756

Chassis No: 5   Engine No: 1   Registered: October 1921

This is the oldest Bentley in existence with chassis No 5 and engine No 1. It was completed at the works in September 1921, the fifth production car. For a short time it was driven by F.T. Burgess who helped 'W.O.' with the design work. It was then handed over to A.F.C. Hillstead, who was sales manager, for him to use as a demonstration car. It is fortunate that such a fine piece of motoring history is still with us today, and in good working order after over fifty-five years. It is now in the collection of Fuad Majzub, who uses it as transport to Bentley Drivers Club meetings.

A.F.C. Hillstead complained about the car when he first took it over from F.T. Burgess as it had a very skimpy four-seater body with no doors. This was not to his liking and when the 1922 TT racing body was being designed he ordered an extra one to be fitted to MD 9756. The polished aluminium body was scratch-finished and varnished, the wings and chassis were painted pillar-box red. To improve performance the engine was fitted with 'W.O's own TT induction manifold and Claudel-Hobson carburettor. In this form it was used by Hillstead for hill climbs and races as well as for sales demonstrations. After 30,000 miles (48,300km) without a single mechanical failure it was sold by the works to a Mr T. Lethbridge. At this time the latest Smith's five-jet carburettor and standard induction manifold was fitted. After having several more owners she was eventually displayed on loan at the Measham Motor Museum. On the closing of this museum MD 9756 was acquired by Mr J.C. Lock, who set about completely overhauling the car and restoring it to as near original condition as possible. At the 1969 Golden Jubilee of Bentley Motors Ltd old No 5 had the honour of carrying W.O. Bentley, then eighty years old, round the other Bentleys gathered together at Oulton Park race circuit for the occasion. Mr J.C. Lock later sold the car to Fuad Majzub of Worcestershire, England.

Above right: Instrument grouping.

Below: Tail view.

Facing page:

Top left: Full front view.

Top right: Engine with TT induction manifold and Claudel-Hobson carburettor.

Below: The oldest Bentley in existence.

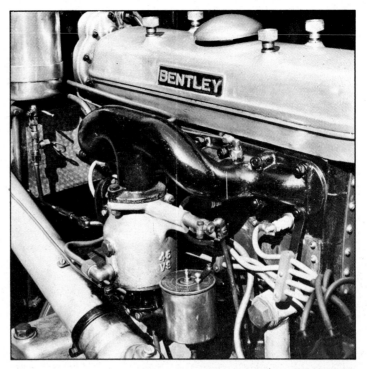

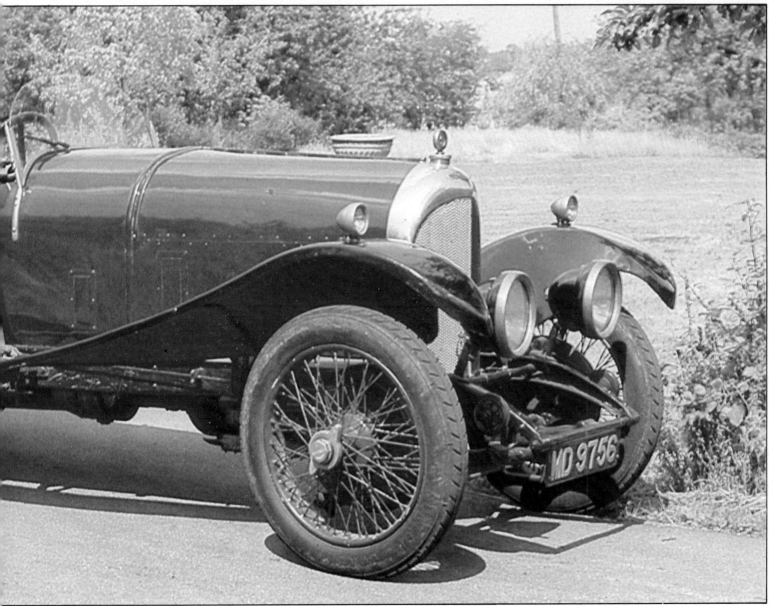

3-Litre BWD467

One of the early 3-litre cars, delivered in February 1922, originally fitted with an all-weather body built by R. Harrison & Sons. The first registration was in Manchester and the owner was Dr Smalley whose address was given as High Street, Manchester. As far as can be traced, he owned the car until 1933 as it was serviced at the works under his name until then – the original registration number is not known. Dr Smalley had front-wheel brakes fitted, probably late in 1924, and 21in well-base wheels fitted in the late 1920s.

Sometime in 1934 in a new owner's 'care' it was crashed quite severely, the main damage being to the body and the chassis which was cracked. After a rebuild, with a replacement chassis, it was re-registered as a new car on 17 December 1937 as BWD 467 by its new owner C. Chester Smith of Redditch. Mr Smith kept the car until the late 1940s. It then had three more owners before being bought in July 1960 by the present owner Mr Ian Douglas, who now says that he had acquired a perfectly 'clapped' green Bentley which he thought was original, but it became his everyday transport for six years. In 1966 a decision had to be made – sell or rebuild? The latter choice was taken, so he sold his pedal bike for £9 and bought a 'B' type gearbox for £7. Ian Douglas then began a collecting campaign amongst members of the Bentley Drivers Club until he had a complete 3-litre in kit form. When assembled he ran the chassis for three years without a body. A new body was built and completed in 1973.

Top left and right: On the road.

Bottom: At a Bentley Drivers Club meeting at Keswick in 1974.

Facing page:

BWD 467 parked at a Bentley meeting in 1977.

3-Litre SY1791

One of the best-kept Bentleys in the world, this lovely car, with a saloon body built by Gurney Nutting, was owned by Miss Ann Knights who lives in Norfolk, England. It was Bentley Drivers Club Champion and best 3-litre saloon between 1972 and 1976. Originally this car had a brakeless front axle and is unique in that the dynamo drive cover is bolted to the bulkhead flange and not to the bulkhead itself. These pictures are a tribute to a beautiful car, which is now owned by Mr J.D.B. Zeal of Surrey, England.

Following spread: SY 1791.

3-Litre CA6600

First owned by Mr King of Colwyn Bay in North Wales, CA 6600 is now owned by Mr Bernard W. Payne of Retford, England. It is fitted with a four-door all-weather tourer by William Arnold of Manchester, with sliding windows to the passenger doors and a wind-up window to the driver's door. This car which has a 10ft 10½in (3.31m) chassis originally cost £1,675 as a complete car. It still retains its original features both bodily and mechanically, and has not been modified in any way.

Below left: Bentley 'B' with blue background.

Below right: Large and rather powerful side light.

Bottom: CA 6600 outside its owner's house.

Facing page:

Above left: Torpedo ventilators.

Above right: Mechanical headlamp dipping – in dipped position.

Below: A neat rear end showing two back 'windows' in hood.

3-Litre XU2472

Chassis No: 655 Engine No: 668 Registered: July 1924

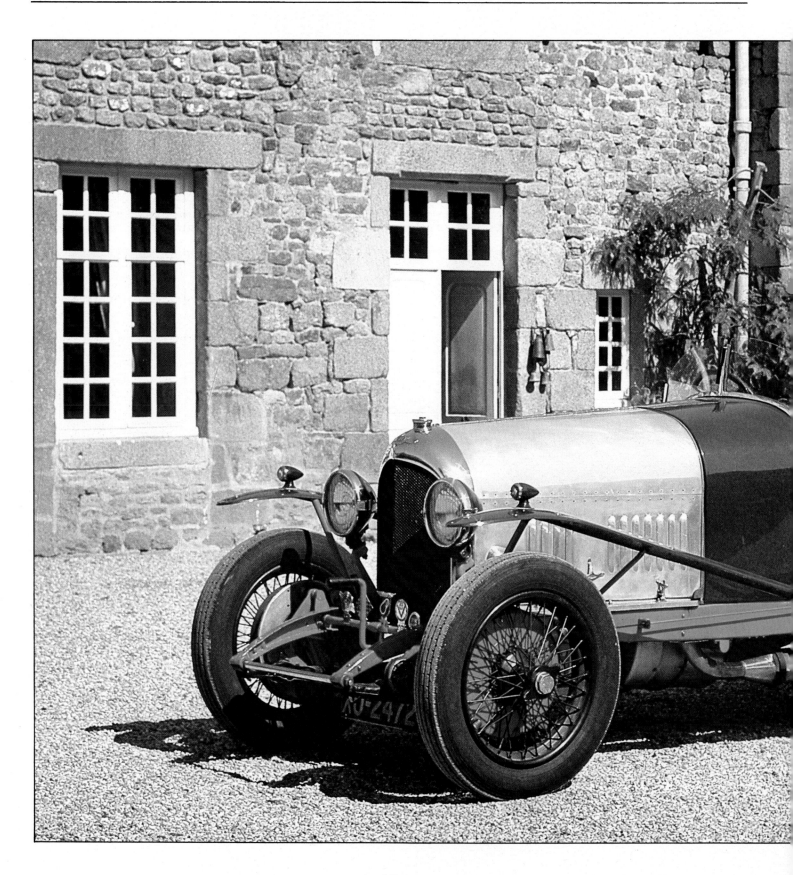

XU 2472 probably had a four-seater touring body on it when supplied to the first owner Major-General Sir George Kemball. Ultimately the car came into the possession of Mr Peter Rae in March 1967 in a very delapidated state. He has rebuilt it into a very pretty two-seater. It was acquired in July 1977 by José Ochoa, a South American enthusiast from Colombia who now lives in London. Since then it has covered over 12,000 miles (19,308km).

Left and below: On a Bentley Drivers Club Tour of Brittany in September 1977.

Bottom: The neat design of the spare-wheel cover.

3-Litre SA8064

Chassis No: 880   Engine No: 894   Registered: April 1925

Chassis number 880 was delivered to the bodybuilders, G.W. Georgeson of Broomhill, Aberdeen, late in 1924. It subsequently had five owners and finally appeared in 1970 in a state of complete ruin at Wolverhampton where the present owner, Mr R.V. Roberts acquired it in April 1971.

An unusual type of body was decided upon, a boat-back style which was in favour in the 1920s. For this particular car, the Thrupp & Maberly Game Hunting Car built in 1926 for the Nawab of Bhopal was thought to be an interesting one to imitate. After some 3,000 hours' work by the owner the car was completed, and since taking to the road in 1973 it has travelled a further 15,000 miles.

Features of particular interest in the car, in addition to the unusual body style, are in the reproduction to original specifications in respect of instrumentation, diamond-buttoned upholstery, Auster windscreens to both front and rear, 21in wheels and hand-forged running-board irons. The early Smith's starter and dynamo are still fitted. A 1939 alteration to the car, the 4½-litre radiator constructed of German nickel silver was considered worth keeping, since it would have an infinite capacity for dealing with overheating in local traffic conditions.

The car is finished to almost concours condition with blue fabric body and sultana brown leather, on the standard that machinery should be right and look right, and the SU Sloper carburettors fitted to it as a 1927 modification are typical of the superb quality that is to be found in the Vintage Bentley.

The long standard 10ft 10in (3.302m) chassis has a B-type gearbox, which employs fairly low, wide-spaced gear ratios, and it has a final drive rear axle of 3.533 (15/53) fitted by the present owner.

Top right: As acquired in April 1971.

Middle right: Touring Brittany, 1976.

Lower right: Engine with twin SU Sloper carburettors.

Below: Back view showing Auster screen to single rear seat.

Facing page: SA 8064 on the road.

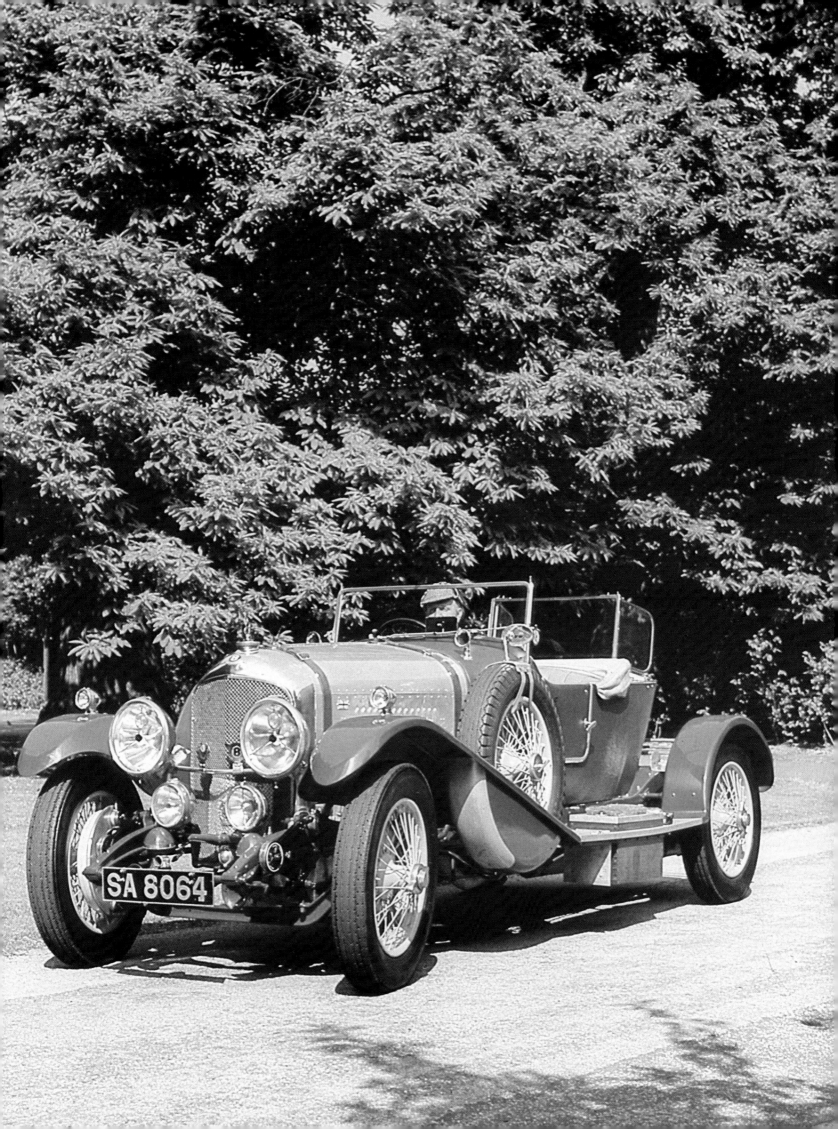

3-Litre BW8619

The Hon Mountjoy Fayne purchased this car in 1927, and it had five further owners up to 1966, of whom the last kept the car for some fifteen years.

The chassis has the A-type close-ratio gearbox normally fitted to these models and the two-seater body has an unusual rounded bob-tail, with a dickey seat or luggage compartment fitting snugly under a two-door lid.

The present owner, Mr David Dalton, bought the car in 1966 for the princely sum of £1,250, and since then has derived considerable pleasure from both working on and driving the car. In addition to the usual refurbishing of the car, he has fitted a 3.53:1 crown wheel and pinion, which gives a comfortable 65mph (104.6 km/h) cruising speed at about 2,500rpm.

In addition to everyday motoring, the car has carried the owner all over Great Britain, to the various weekend functions arranged by the Bentley Drivers Club, of which he is a keen member.

Some time early in its fifty-two-year life it has had an engine change, and Number 451 is the number recorded on the existing one, which would appear to have come from a 1923 car.

Top right: A rear view rather like a bumble bee.

Middle right: Open single rear or 'Mother-in-Law' seat.

Below: BW 8619 is an impressive car from the front.

Facing page: A page from the service department records.

A. 7 Rutter. 89 West Arthur St S.W.

Engine 1037. 14/53 axle ratio 1925 Speed G.E. 4 4.30
Short Change Speed lever. best Hand Brake Liners. Greaser
front end of dynamo. Tecalemit greaser to front Universal jo
Crankshaft slotted for fan drive. Steering at lowest possible r
Clutch stop fitted. Cambridge Thermometer, A.T. rev counter. Sing
slot B.H.B. H.C. Pistons. 1925.

15.6. Top vertical bevels adjusted. Chassis lubricated throughout. Minor adjustm
26.7. Minor adjustments 23.9. Minor adjustments 17.10. Rattle in control tubes rectified
28.9. lines in vertical shaft & cylinder block sealed. 30.11. 820 x 120 Rudge Whitworth wheel fitted
15.12. Front brake liners cleaned off & roughed up. 5.3. B.H.B. H.C. pistons fitted. Piston rings ne
10.5. camshaft fitted. Top vertical bevels renewed & adjusted. Units sealed 30.12. Off side
springs changed
1926
9.2. Heavy petrol consumption rectified. Twin S.U. carburetters changed. 20. New electrodes fit
Sparking Plugs on inlet side. 14.5. Tap in overhead gear rectified. Slack in propshaft universal joints taken up. St
column wandering rectified 6.7. New large type water pump fitted. B type gearbox fitted. Lift in steering box tak
foot brakes relined. hand & foot brakes recompensated & adjusted. Units sealed 6.9. New 820 x 120 wheels fitted. New
Slow Running type carburetters fitted 30.9. Engine decarbonised. Shackle bolts & brushes renewed. New silenc
chamber complete. A type gearbox fitted 2. New o/s front wheel New set of J.D. Sparking Plugs. Carburetters clea
4.10. Silencer fish tail fitted 12.10. Radiator repaired 19.10. 8 leaf front road springs fitted. O/s rear Hartford S.D. da
8.11. Cylinder block removed. Pistons lapped in. Units sealed 8.11. Steering wobble rectified

1927.

8.2. New large type water pump fitted 22.2. Flywheel teeth repaired. 10.6. Sent for transfer of guar
Hon. Mountjoy Fane. Holywell Hall. Stamford.
16.9. Sent for transfer of guarantee. 1928.
30.12. Transfer of guar. Starter teeth rounded up. Slack in rear universal joint taken up. Starter motor cl

Stanley Robinson. Kinwarton House. Alcester

1928.

Webb
1.8.W.T. New blocks & slippers fitted to rear universal. New races fitted on pinion shaft. Teeth meshe

1929.

18.4. 16 valves & guides sent to Henry Garner Ltd.

1933

22.9. Long + 2 short pins + 4 brushes for front universal joint sent to County Garage. Barn

1934.

3.7. spring shackle + 14T bevel pinion sent to W. Lawsk, Auto Eng. Aberdeen

3-Litre NR6714

Chassis No: 1072   Engine No: 1084   Registered: July 1925

NR 6714 is one of a fleet of Bentleys owned by Mr J.D. Smith who lives in Somerset, England. Supplied new with a Vanden Plas four-seater touring body, it was considerably rebuilt in 1958, since when it has won many awards for its present owner. The car has an A type gearbox and twin SU Sloper carburettors.

Below: NR 6714 parked in the drive of the owner's home.

Facing page:

Top left: At Dartmouth Royal Naval College in June 1967.

Top right: At Silverstone.

32

3-Litre YL5778

Chassis No: 1191   **Engine No: 1202**   **Registered: October 1925**

This Speed Model supplied new to F. Fenwick Luke of London still has its original Vanden Plas four-seater touring body. The car suffered an accident in 1932 and was rebuilt on a new frame. It was owned for some years since the war by Mr Dennis Miller-Williams who sold it to the present owner, Mr David Llewellyn of Eastbourne.

Right: YL 5778 on a Scottish Rally near Aviemore.

Below: When owned by Mr Dennis Miller-Williams YL 5778 was painted black with red frames.

Facing page:

Top: In her present colour scheme YL 5778 is seen shortly after being judged Champion and Best Vintage Bentley at Kensington Gardens in 1975.

Bottom: Spit and polish in the engine-room.

3-Litre YN8369

Built in 1926, and fitted from new with a standard Vanden Plas body, it was bought in 1936 for Mr Norman Hood by his father for £150, after it had changed hands about five times in the previous ten years. The original wings had been replaced by 'Le Mans' type. It was run in this form until the end of the war, but the 3-litre engine dropped a valve, and was replaced by a 4½-litre from a scrap Gurney Nutting saloon, registration No YV 5471, with engine No MF 3167.

After about 100,000 miles, the engine suffered the misfortune of a broken con-rod, and the Bentley was laid up. Twelve years later, Norman Hood decided that the modern pressed-steel car lacked that certain something, and a yearning to relive earlier motoring days made him decide to rebuild the Bentley. This commenced around 1962 and took five years to complete, the entire work being carried out by the owner.

The rebuilt car can be easily distinguished by its slim, lithe appearance and one of the many points of interest is the superb petrol tank, built in copper, of soldered and riveted construction, typical of the high standard of workmanship evident on the whole of the car, it is finished in British racing green with grey leather.

In 1971, the car in the hands of Mr Hood began an active three years of competition motoring, during which it achieved various degrees of success.

Right: Steering wheel and instrument layout.

Below: YN 8369 is an impressive car from a low angle.

Facing page:

Top left: Completed chassis awaiting body in 1964.

Top right: Waiting starter's orders at the Mas du Clos Circuit near Aubusson, France, 1970.

Below: Rear view showing copper petrol tank.

Following spread: YN 8369.

3-Litre YR5748

Chassis No: AH 1483 **Engine No: AH 1482** **Registered: June 1926**

This car, still bearing its original two-seater drop-head body by Surbiton Coach and Motor Works of Surbiton, Surrey, England, was first owned by Brigadier-General N. Bicket. After changing hands many times it is now part of the Fuad Majzub collection. At the present time the car is awaiting a complete overhaul. The photograph at the right shows the headlamps in the dipped position.

3-Litre YH3197

The first owner of this car was Mr C.A. Ackner of London, who chose this four-door Weymann-type saloon body built by J. Gurney Nutting & Co Ltd, of Chelsea, London. After about twelve months Mr Ackner decided to have the car modified by fitting a Wilson pre-selector gearbox which still remains on the car.

It is now owned by Mr R.L. Rolt of Worcestershire, England. The picture on the left shows the instrument layout, the one below, the headlamp dipping lever, the gear pre-selector and the handbrake.

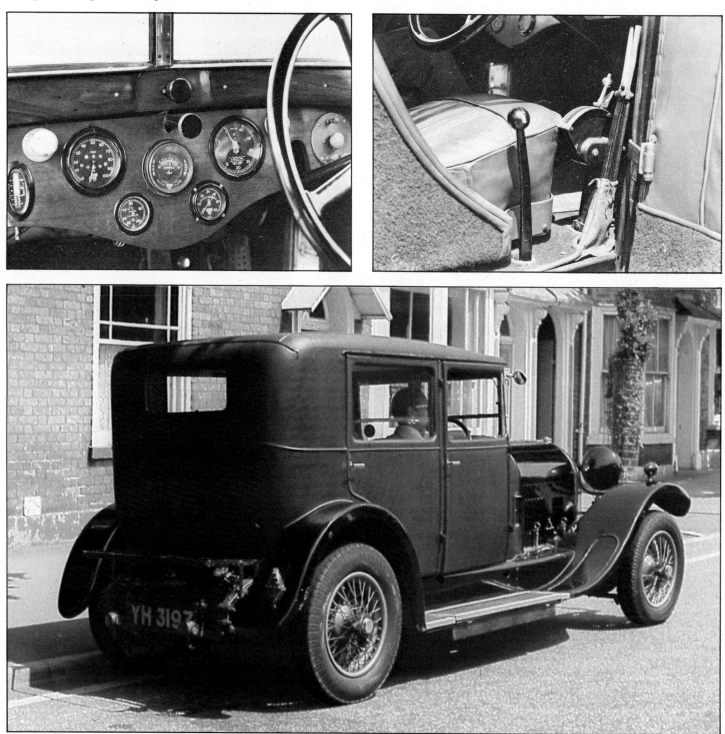

6½-Litre & Speed Six

1925 saw the entry into the motoring world, of the 6½-litre, a 'W.O.' masterpiece, developed from experiments on a 4½-litre capacity six-cylinder engine. The new engine was fitted into a massive new chassis strengthened with one tube and four pressed-steel cross-members, intended to carry heavy luxury bodywork, which, of course, the 3-litre was unable to do without an unacceptable loss of performance. A cruising speed of 75mph (120km/h) was well within the capabilities of the new car.

Few companies achieved fame, both national and international, as quickly as did Bentley Motors. This was due to the fact that the new models produced proved immediately satisfactory and needed hardly any modifications – a reflection of the tradition of sound basic design combined with the use of quality materials. The standard 6½-litre was offered with a wheelbase of 11ft (3.35m), 12ft (3.66m), or 12ft 6in (3.80m), although one 11ft 6in (3.51m) and one 12ft 8½in (3.87m) chassis are known to have been made. However, modifications were subsequently made to cure minor steering problems and with later type front springs (BM5899) the repositioned axle gave wheelbases of 11ft 1¼in (3.38m), 12ft 1¼in (3.69m) and 12ft 7¼in (3.84m). The engine followed the normal Bentley practice of four tulip-shaped valves per cylinder and was fed from a single Smith updraught carburettor. The overhead camshaft was driven by a remarkable system, consisting of two tiny three-throw eccentrics, coupled by triple connecting rods, with the drive coming from a helical gear taken from the rear of the crankshaft, a device said to reflect Doncaster locomotive practice. The crankshaft had the refinement of a multi-disc torsional damper which proved very effective. The compression ratio was 4.4:1.

The water-pump and dynamo were driven from the front and rear of the camshaft, respectively, and it derived considerable damping from these units. Ignition was by twin magnetos to two plugs per cylinder; later, in 1927, this was changed to a coil and magneto. It was believed to be the first motor car engine to be mounted flexibly on rubber blocks, and helped to transmit the superb smooth output. A new clutch mechanism was adopted to activate the single-plate clutch, the two normal rollers being substituted by two small links operating long levers. The rear axle was a semi-floating type and was offered with either a 3.8 or 4.1 final drive, fitted into a re-designed axle casing; a more robust, longer axle nose-piece was used to take the extra torque. The drive was passed through a modified gearbox which had fairly high gear ratios, including a third gear of 1.278:1, the highest ever used by 'W.O.' in any standard Bentley that he built.

Below: An illustration from the 1928 6½-litre catalogue showing a Pullman Limousine de Ville which cost £2,800.

Facing page: An artist's impression of a 6½-litre on an Alpine pass from the 1928 catalogue.

The 1927 Motor Show saw early modifications including the fitting of a Dewandre Servo, and the now familiar dynamo driven from the front of the crankshaft and snugly fitted into the bottom edge of a modified and deeper radiator; a torsional damper was fitted to the camshaft a little later. The road speed at 3,500rpm was 84mph (135.14km/h) in fourth gear, and a *Motor* road-test report, dated 21 September 1926, quoted a top-gear performance of 10 to 65mph (16 to 104.58km/h) in 30 seconds, carrying an all up weight of 2 tons 8 cwts (2,438.40kg), including driver and two passengers. This top-gear performance of the car was remarkable for its flexibility. Steady demand was found for the new car, and 363 chassis were produced between 1926 and 1930, the last delivery recorded being in November 1930.

In October 1928 the Speed Six appeared at Olympia. It was a tuned and developed version of the standard car with twin carburettors. The model was easily identified by the parallel-sided radiator and the green background of the badge, whereas the sides of the standard radiator tapered inwards at the bottom, and a blue background to the Bentley 'B'. The car was built on either 11ft 6in (3.51m), 11ft 8½in (3.57m) or 12ft 8½in (3.87m) wheelbases, although the specially prepared Le Mans team cars had a short 11ft (3.35m) wheelbase chassis. Later, some cars were fitted with modified front springs (BM 6907) and a repositioned front axle beam increased wheelbases by 2½in (63.5mm) so that most designed 11ft 6in (3.51m) cars would have ended up with a 11ft 8½in (3.57m) wheelbase.

The first Speed Six prepared especially for Le Mans, in 1929 on chassis No LB 2332, had many engine and chassis modifications. One interesting innovation was a foot-operated horn button fitted

to the floor by the side of the clutch pedal, which kept the driver's hands free for the business of steering a winning path around the circuit. This car won the 1929 race and another 6½ won again in 1930; co-driver of the winning car in both years was Woolf Barnato. The 1929 Le Mans result was the first win by a Speed Six, the first Rudge-Whitworth Biennial Cup win, and Bentley's fourth win at that famous race circuit in the Sarthe, since the 24-hour race was first run there in May 1923. The 1929 show models (KR Series) incorporated many engine modifications developed as a result of racing, including the single-port cylinder block and induction manifold, strengthened shell-type connecting rod bearings, and Elektron steering-box and rear axle casing; a 5 gallon (22.75 litres) Elektron sump was fitted, and an increased compression ratio used.

Between 1929 and 1930, 182 Speed Six chassis were built, many equipped with beautifully proportioned bodies which complemented the stupendous performance of which the cars were capable. It is generally accepted that the Speed Six was 'W.O.'s favourite car.

SPECIFICATION

6½-LITRE

In production from 1926 to 1930

Basic specification at time of introduction (with some later production modifications):

ENGINE

6 cylinders; firing order 1, 4, 2, 6, 3, 5.

Bore	3.94in (100mm)
Stroke	5.51in (140mm)
Capacity	6,597cc (402.4cu in)
Compression ratio	4.4:1
Brake horsepower	140 (at 3,200rpm)
RAC rating	37.2hp

Valves and camshaft

Four valves per cylinder. Tulip-shaped operated by rear-driven

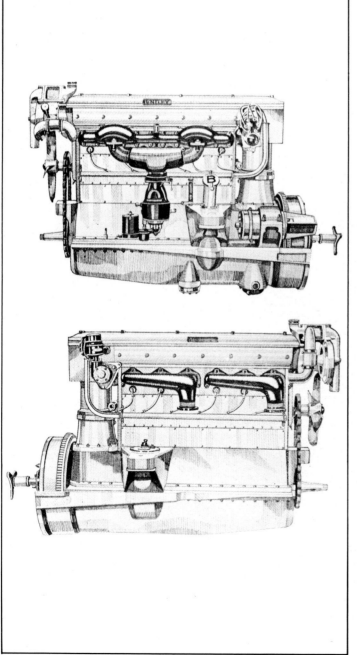

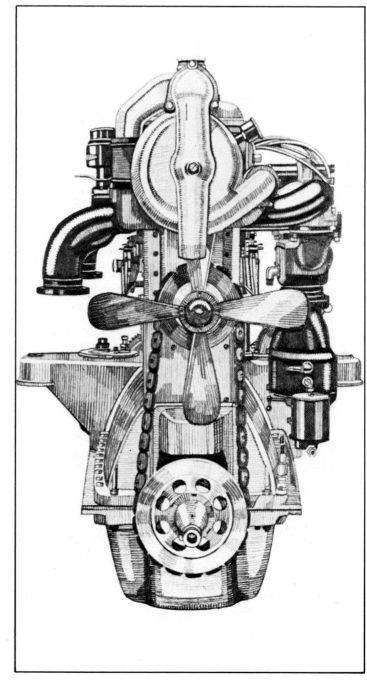

46

(triple-rod) single overhead camshaft running in eight bearings. Camshaft damper fitted in 1927.

Cylinder block and pistons
Non-detachable head en bloc in cast-iron with BHB silent type pistons.

Crankcase and sump
Cast aluminium alloy and one-piece sump.

Crankshaft
Mounted in eight white metal bearings with vibration damper fixed at front end. Two-bolt con-rods with direct metal bearings.

Lubrication
Pressure feed to main bearings, big ends and overhead gear, splash to pistons and gudgeon pins. Sump capacity 3 gallons (13.65 litres).

Ignition
Twin synchronised magnetos (ML/GR6 or ER6) up to 1927 then one magneto and alternative coil (Delco Remy MR7 with distribu-

tor fitted to off side). Sparking plugs two per cylinder, KLG J1/K1 or Lodge CV-18mm.

Carburettors
Single Smith updraught type BVS50 (five-jet) later single Smith-Bentley type 50 BVS—both manifold and carburettor heated by water jackets. Ki-gass pump for cold starting.

Dynamo
Smith 2DAC5—constant current with cutout, driven from front of crankshaft by two 'Hardy' joints. Early cars (1926-27) had dynamo driven from rear of camshaft. 12 volt.

Starter
Smiths 4LSA with Smith's starter switch.

Instruments
'Telegauge' on petrol tank. Smith's bezel switch and ammeter, AT (later Jaeger) speedometer, oil pressure gauge.

Cooling system
Forced pump circulation with thermostat control and belt driven fan. Capacity $7\frac{1}{4}$ gallons (32.99 litres).

Petrol system
Autovac capacity 8 pints (4.55 litres), rear tank, early models 19 gallons (86.45 litres) including 3 gallon (13.7 litres) reserve. Later, 25 gallons (113.75 litres).

TRANSMISSION
Gearbox
Four forward speeds and reverse with positive interlock right-hand gate change 'BS' type. Oil capacity six pints (3.42 litres).
  Ratios: BS type gearbox: Reverse, 3.364:1; First, 3.364:1; Second, 1.823:1; Third, 1.278:1; Top, direct.
  The C type gearbox was occasionally fitted.
Oil capacity: 6 pints (3.42 litres).

Clutch
Single dry plate, halo lined. 1927 spring-loaded pressure plate used.

Propeller shaft
One-piece open shaft with plunging (or 'pot') joints lubricated by grease nipple, later (1928) Hardy Spicer joints.

Rear Axle and Final Drive
Semi-floating underslung spiral bevel (four bevel pinion differential) giving engine to road wheel ratios in top 13/46 (3.538:1) early models; 13/50 (3,846:1); 12/50 (4.1:1).
  Oil capacity 3 pints (1.71 litres).

CHASSIS
Frame
Deep 'U'-section, four pressed-steel cross-members and one large tubular cross-member at front of rear springs, gauge 0.156in (4mm); later cars 0.188in (5mm).

Suspension
Semi-elliptic front and rear, three spring specifications were offered depending on wheelbase and type of body. Spring gaiters were fitted.

Shock absorbers
Bentley and Draper Duplex (size 3 at front and size 4 at rear) or Hartford Duplex (Silentbloc bushes in clamps). Later Bentley and

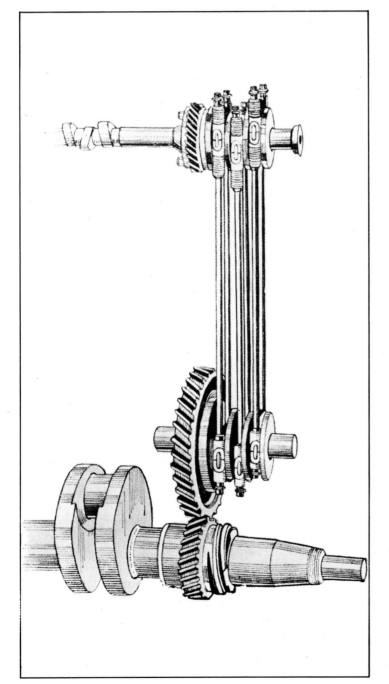

Left: Four drawings from the 6½-litre catalogue showing the engine and method of driving the overhead camshaft via three-throw eccentrics and triple connecting rods.

BENTLEY
SIX·AND·A·HALF LITRE
SIX·CYLINDER
STANDARD MODEL

BENTLEY MOTORS LTD.

Showrooms:
POLLEN HOUSE, CORK STREET, LONDON, W.1
Telephones: Regent 6911 (3 lines)

REGISTERED OFFICES & WORKS: SERVICE DEPARTMENT: KINGS·
OXGATE LANE, CRICKLEWOOD,   BURY LANE, THE HYDE, HENDON,
LONDON, N.W.2.   &   LONDON, N.W.9
TELEPHONE: WILLESDEN 2140   TELEPHONE: COLINDALE 6371

Telegrams to all Departments: Bennotlim, Phone, London

DIRECTORS:
H'olf Barnato
Ramsay Manners, W. O. Bentley,
J. K. Carruth   H. Pike,
Marquis de Casa Maury (Cuban)

The title page of the October 1928 catalogue.

Draper single short-arm dampers at front and Bentley-Draper lever type hydraulic at rear.

Brakes
Footbrake, four-wheel mechanical push-rod to front. Internal expanding 16in (406mm) drums with balance beam compensator with front Perrot shafts. Handbrake on separate shoes to rear wheels only. Later models (1927) had Dewandre servo-assisted Self-wrapping front brakes.

Front axle
'H'-section 40-ton tensile steel. 1930 heavy type axle bed.

Steering
Worm and wheel type, ratio 13.75:1. 18in (457.2mm) diameter steering wheel with three angles of rake available for steering column.

Exhaust System
Two separate manifolds (three cylinders each) leading to two exhaust pipes into a single expansion chamber followed by silencer and single tailpipe fitted with cast-iron fishtail.

Wheels
Rudge-Whitworth, detachable wire, centre locking with left and right hand threads.

Tyres
Early cars 6.25in x 33in (158mm x 838mm) semi-balloon, later 6.25in x 21in (158mm x 533mm) Dunlop Cord balloon.

PRINCIPAL CHASSIS DETAILS AND DIMENSIONS
Wheelbase: 11ft (3.35m) early cars only. 12ft (3.66m) or 12ft 6in (3.81m) (later both were increased by 1½in (38mm)).
Track: 4ft 8in (1.42m).
Overall length: 15ft 1in (4.6m) early cars only. 16ft 1in (4.9m) or 16ft 7in (5.06m).
Overall body width: 5ft 8½in (1.74m).
Turning circle: Right 51ft (15.55m) or 55ft (16.76m), Left 50ft (15.24m) or 54ft (16.46m).
Ground clearance: 9in (229mm).
Weight: Chassis 32½cwt (1,638kg) or 33cwt (1,663kg). With open body 42cwt (2,117kg) to 45cwt (2,268kg).
Performance: Maximum speed 84mph (135.2kph) at 3,500rpm with 12/50 axle. Petrol consumption 10-14mpg.
Price at introduction: Chassis £1,450 – 1928 (12ft 7½in) £1,575 Complete car (11ft) Weyman saloon £2,050. Comparison price Rolls-Royce 40/50 £1,850-1,900.

Number built: 363.
Radiator badge: Blue enamel background.

SPECIFICATION

SPEED-SIX

In production 1929-30.

Basic specification as for 6½-litre except for the following variations:

ENGINE
Compression ratio 5.1:1; later (1930) 5:3.1.
Brake horsepower 160 (at 3,500rpm); 180 (single port block)

Cylinder block and pistons
Single inlet port, later models two ports. BHB pistons.

Crankcase and sump
Later models had large 5 gallon (22.75 litres) Elektron sump fitted.

Crankshaft
Later cars plus $\frac{5}{16}$in (8mm) radius. Maximum safe revolutions 3,500rpm.

Ignition
Magneto Bosch type FU6B or MLGR6 and coil, Delco Remy MRS1Z. 12 volt electrics from 2 x 6 volt Young batteries. Sparking plugs: two per cylinder – KLG type 417 or Champion 18mm.

Carburettors
Twin SU vertical type HVGS (to near side).

Starter
Some later cars had Bosch BNEZ/12 RS2 (co-axial).

Instruments
Jaeger revolution counter and speedometer, Smith thermometer, Hobson petrol gauge, Smith bezel switch and Delco switch box, Smith oil gauge. Later cars: clock, Hobson rectangular petrol gauge, revolution counter, and Weston ammeter.

Cooling system
Capacity 54 pints (30.7 litres).

Petrol system
25 gallons (113.8 litres).

TRANSMISSION
Gearbox
Nearly all cars had 'C'-type, only a few had 'D'-type.
    'D'-type ratios: Reverse, 2.64:1; First, 2.64:1; Second, 1.63:1;
        Third, 1.35:1; Top, direct.

Propeller shaft
One-piece open shaft with Hardy Spicer joints.

Rear axle and final drive
As standard 6½-litre with ratios 13/50 (3.846:1); 13/46 (3.538:1);
or 15/50 (3.3:1).

CHASSIS
Shock absorbers
As later 6½-litres.

Brakes
As 6½-litre with Dewandre vacuum, servo assistance. Aluminium
brake shoes with halo linings.

Steering
Later models had Elektron steering box. 18in (457mm) diameter
steering wheel.

Exhaust
Two separate manifolds leading to single exhaust pipe, silencer and
tailpipe.

Tyres
6.75in x 18in (171.5mm x 457mm).
6in x 33in (152.4mm x 838mm) by special order – Goodrich medium
                                pressure.
6in x 21in (152.4mm x 533mm) or 6.75in x 21in (171.5mm x
533mm).

Miscellaneous
Detachable stoneguard fitted to radiator; Lucas P100 DB headlamps.

PRINCIPAL CHASSIS DETAILS AND DIMENSIONS
Wheelbase: 11ft 6in (3.51m), later 11ft 8½in (3.57m) or 12ft 8½in
       (3.87m).
Overall length: 15ft 7in (4.75m) and 16ft 7in (5.06m).
Turning circle: Right 48ft 6in (14.78m); Left 47ft 6in (14.48m);
       with 11ft 6in (3.51m) chassis.
Weight: Chassis (11ft 8½in; 3.56m) 33cwt (1,663kg) or 35cwt
       (1,764kg) with equipment.
       With open body 42cwt (1,663kg).
Performance: Maximum speed 92mph (148km/h) with 13/46
       back axle.
       Petrol consumption 11mpg.
Number built: 182.
Price at introduction: £1,700. Complete car Weyman-Gurney
                Nutting £2,315.
Radiator badge: Green enamel.

**Below: The Speed Six engine with Twin SU vertical HVGS
type carburettors.**

7995.

6½-Litre YV2525

Chassis No: BR 2355   Engine No: BR 2354   Registered: March 1928

YV 2525 is a real enthusiast's car, which started life as a more stately carriage. First registered on 28 March 1928, it was fitted with a four-door four-light saloon by Weymann's Motor Bodies (1925) Ltd of Addlestone in Surrey, one of only fourteen Bentley 6½-litre chassis for which they built bodies.

This car was a standard 12ft 6in (3.81m) wheelbase chassis number BR 2355 and engine BR 2354, and was initially used as a London demonstration car before being sold to a Mr William Bastard from Leicestershire later in 1929, and it stayed in this area with one other owner until 1969 when it was purchased by the present owner, Mr George Tabbenor of Staffordshire, England.

Despite the very pleasant saloon body which was still in reasonable condition, the new owner had set his heart on an open tourer as he wished eventually to use the car for competitions. The car was therefore completely stripped down and a major rebuild carried out. The first job was to shorten the chassis by 18 inches (450mm) to 11ft 0in (3.35m), the same wheelbase as adopted for the works competition cars. A replica Vanden Plas four-seater tourer body was built, with a Le Mans type 48-gallon (218.5-litre) petrol tank. The 21in (533mm) wheels were replaced with 19in (482mm) and Dunlop racing tyres 19 x 600 front and 19 x 700 rear and a 3.33:1 final drive fitted. During the course of the engine rebuild the cylinder block was machined to give a compression ratio of about 6.1 and Speed-Six-type pistons fitted. A special inlet manifold was made to take three 2in (50mm) SU carburettors, replacing the original, to give the car a maximum speed of 110mph (176km/h) after it had been carefully run in. Since the rebuild the car has competed at Shelsley Walsh and the Brighton Speed Trials and has been a regular competitor at Bentley Drivers Club events at Oulton Park and Silverstone. It has also been to Le Mans, and was driven in the 1973 Mille Miglia (1,000 mile – 1,610km) rally, Padua-Rome-Padua, and in the 1974 Swedish Rally of the Lakes. The car and its owner turn out regularly to Bentley Drivers Club events in the Midlands.

Below: While touring Brittany 1977.

Facing page:

Top left: Filling the 48 gallon (218.5 litre) tank.

Centre left: Original saloon body.

Top right: A halt in the 1974 Swedish Rally of the Lakes.

Centre right: The 1973 Mille Miglia.

Bottom: Competing in the Bentley Drivers Club Silverstone Meeting August 1972.

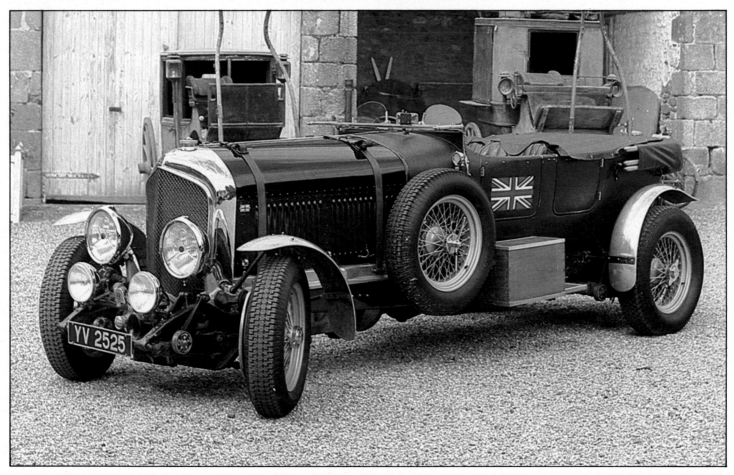

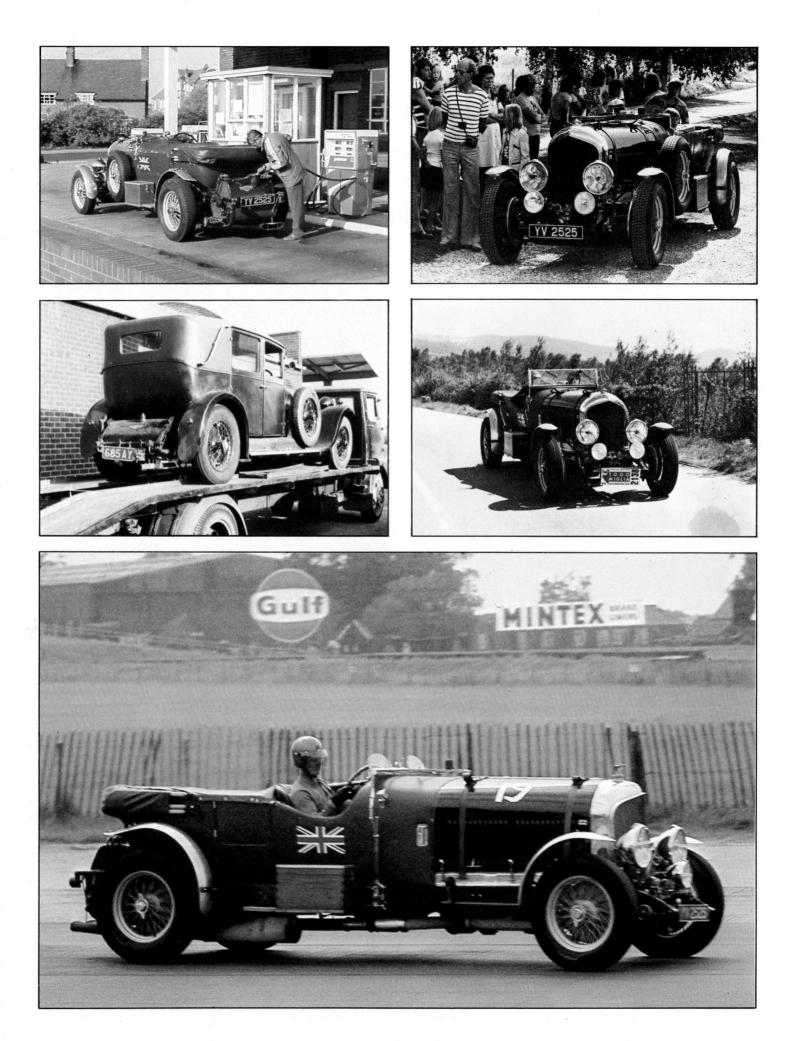

6½-Litre JD9961

Chassis No: KF 2400   Engine No: KF 2400   Registered: July 1929

JD 9961 is one of the very few Barker boat-tail-bodied Bentleys. The first owner of this car was Mr Ralph Jump and the original registration number was PK 9460. The chassis is a Speed Six as befits such a body. This car is now owned by Mr George Milligen of Norfolk, England, and the car was to be seen at a number of Bentley Drivers Club meetings in 1977.

53

6½-Litre UP2224

Chassis No: WT 2271   **Engine No: WT 2762**   **Registered: March 1929**

This car, with drop-head coupé body with dickey seat, built by Motor Bodies (Newcastle) Ltd was supplied to the first owner, Mr Wilfred Blythe, by Frank Scott in Newcastle-upon-Tyne. At some time during its life this car has had an engine change. The original engine was No WT 2273 in a standard chassis, the one now in the car, No SB 2762 came from a Speed Six chassis No KR 2700 which had a registration number UV 8516. The car, which is in concours condition, is owned by Mr R.A. Parker of Nuneaton, England.

6½-Litre UV6605

Chassis No: KR 2678   Engine No: KR 2684   Registered: December 1929

This Speed Six chassis was delivered to the coachbuilders Windovers Ltd of London in October 1929. They built a four-door saloon body on it for the Hon Esmond Harmsworth, who was the first owner. Nothing seems to be known about this car until it was acquired by Mr R.H.A. Coombs in 1951 after which it had three more owners before it was bought in 1959 by Mr M.B. Gaudin, when it was still more or less in original condition. It was last used in saloon form by Mr Gaudin at the Vintage Sports Car Club Meeting at Prescott Hill Climb in 1959, by this time the body had deteriorated very badly and the following year it was removed and scrapped. No immediate rebuild was undertaken, and in this con-

dition it was sold to the present owner Mr R.M.G. Hoare of Stoke Gabriel, Devon, in 1962. Rebuilding in amateur hands is a slow and painstaking process and the chassis was not complete until 1975 when the car went to Barry Simpson Engineering of Newton Abbot in Devon for a new body. This is an open two-seater with dickey, built to the owner's design and was not completed until late in 1976. The resulting hard work has produced a very handsome and worthwhile motor car.

Below: UV 6605 as she is today.

Facing page, top left: In the paddock at Prescott in 1959.

56

6½-Litre UV8639

This Speed Six, still with its original coupé body built by H.J. Mulliner, was supplied to a Mr T.O. Mills. When these photographs were taken at the Welcombe Hotel at Stratford-upon-Avon, England, in 1968 the car was owned by Mr W.D.S. Lake. It is now owned by Mr Johnson of Bletchley, Buckinghamshire.

6½-Litre 873HYV

Chassis No: KR 2687   Engine No: KR 2686   Registered: 1929

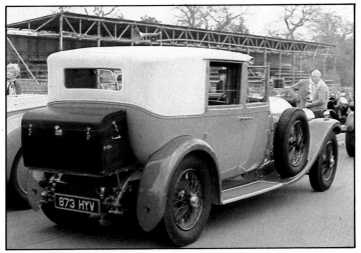

Starting life with registration number GK 3664, was shown at the 1929 Motor Show at Olympia and was bought by a Mr John Davis. It was fitted with a limousine body by H.J. Mulliner Ltd. Now owned by Mr Adrian Garrett, of Australia, who keeps 873 HYV in England.

6½-Litre GJ3811

Chassis No: HM 2855   Engine No: HM 2863   Registered: May 1930

Surely one of the most glamorous Bentleys ever built. Shortly after his win at Le Mans in 1929 with H.R.S. Birkin in a 6½-litre Bentley, Woolf Barnato, who was chairman of Bentley Motors Limited, decided he would like a similar car for his own personal use with a closed body. The 11ft 8½in (3.57m) chassis was chosen and the body built by Gurney Nutting & Co Ltd of Chelsea, on the Weymann principle. To achieve the rakish swept roofline required by Barnato it was necessary to have only one rear seat set in a transverse position, it was luxuriously fitted, complete with cocktail cabinet. The car was completed early in 1930 and Barnato took it on a test run to the south of France. While there, it was decided over lunch that, without a great effort, London could be reached more quickly than by train. On 13 March 1930, with Dale Bourne, a golfing friend, Barnato left Cannes at 6 pm, shortly after the Blue Train began its journey to Calais. They reached Boulogne at 10.30 am on the 14th and embarked on the 11.35 am boat, were in Folkestone soon after one o'clock and came to rest at the RAC in Pall Mall, London, at 3.30 pm, three and three-quarter hours before

the Blue Train passengers reached Victoria Station. They had never exceeded 75mph (120km/h) and averaged 43.43mph (69.5km/h) across France. Shortly after this, surely the longest pre-delivery settling-down run on record, GJ 3811 was duly registered on 21 May 1930.

Among the early owners of the car were Lord Brougham and Vaux, and Charles Mortimer of Brooklands Outer Circuit fame. For many years before it was bought by its present owner Mr H.N. Harben it had lain in a timber garage in the Midlands and had become very dilapidated. A complete rebuild took three years, during which the chassis, engine, body and trim were completely refurbished, much of the work being done personally by its new owner. Outward alterations from the original were minimal: a slightly deepened windscreen and back window, and a Webasto sliding roof. The colour was also changed from black to British racing green.

GJ 3811 has a 'C'-type gearbox, and has been restored to its original specification except that Hugh Harben has fitted high-

compression pistons 6.6:1 of his own manufacture, together with a 3.3:1 final drive axle, the same ratio as that used by the works when racing in 1929 and 1930. A vacuum reservoir has also been added for the brake servo. The car is still capable of considerably more than 100mph (160km/h) and has competed at Silverstone and Shelsley Walsh, but with a total weight exceeding 2½ tons (12,320kg) and a fuel consumption of only 10mpg (3.5km per litre) it has obvious limitations. The car has covered over 20,000 miles (32,200 km) since being rebuilt, has been driven to Le Mans and taken round the famous circuit and is reputed to be among the most valuable vintage cars in the UK. It is still in regular though restricted use, and is not just a museum piece.

Right: The compact tool kit which stows in the lid of the boot.

Below: This rear view shows the swept roof line and the small rear window, after being enlarged!

Facing page:

Top left: GJ 3811 was a sorry sight when bought by Hugh Harben.

Top right: Captain Woolf Barnato with his car in 1930.

Bottom: GJ 3811 competing in 'The Times' Challenge Trophy at the Bentley Drivers Club meeting at Silverstone in August 1972.

Overleaf: A summer picnic with GJ 3811.

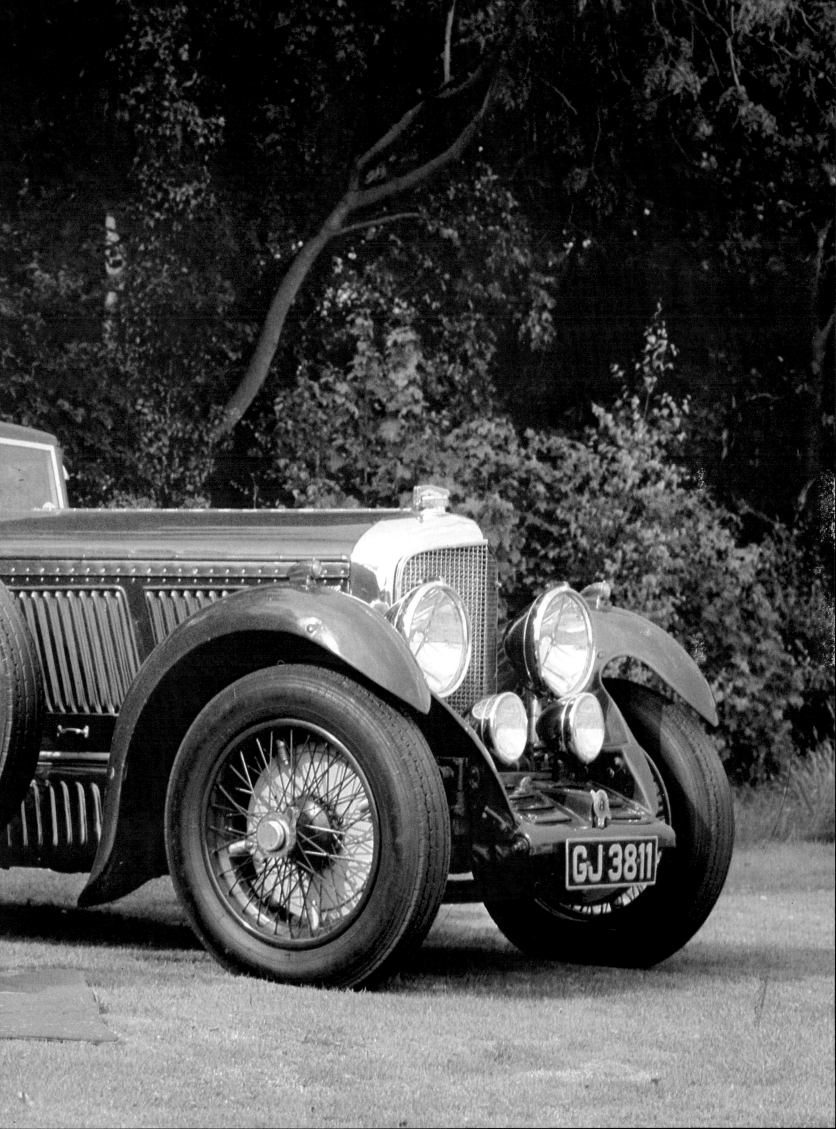

6½-Litre GF8507

Chassis No: HM 2868   Engine No: HM 2872   Registered: May 1930

GF 8507 is one of the famous 6½-litre works team cars, and was the next to last Speed Six built. In June 1930 it finished second at Le Mans in The Grande Prix d'Endurance driven by F.C. Clement and R. Watney, and the month before had won the Junior Car Club's Double Twelve Hour Race at Brooklands, driven by F.C. Clement and Woolf Barnato. After Le Mans the car was sold to a private individual. Very little seems to be known about this car until it was bought by Carl Mueller of Wisconsin, USA in 1950, who drove it in many US vintage car meetings. It is now owned by Dr J.J. Stickley of Iowa, USA.

Below: GF 8507 as she is today.

Facing page:

Top left: The engine-room.

Top right: Dash-board and instrumentation.

Middle: GF 8507 in 1930.

Below: An understanding State Administrator provided the number plate LE MANS for the Team Speed Six to wear. The curious shape of the figure 2 is authentic.

6½-Litre GN5268

Chassis No: NH 2750   **Engine No: LR 2781**   **Registered: July 1930**

GN 5268 is one of the fifty-one Speed Sixes with the 11ft 8½in (3.57m) chassis. The body, which is original, is a four-seater tourer with glass side-screens and was built by R. Harrison & Son. This car is now owned by Dr W.J.R. Pickles, who lives in Yorkshire, England.

6½-Litre TA3855

Chassis No: SB 2755   **Engine No: SB 2766**   **Registered: September 1930**

This Speed Six chassis originally had a Weymann-type coupé body built by James Young & Co Ltd of Bromley, Kent, for Mrs M. Vardy and bore the registration number GF 392. It is now owned by Mr Jack Smith of Somerset, England, who bought it from the Hon James Bruce when it carried the number SMX 158 and still had the coupé body. The present owner has completely rebuilt the car and constructed a replica Vanden Plas four-seater tourer body for it. The picture to the right shows the car with the partly finished tourer body. Since rebuilding TA 3855 was taken on a run to Le Mans in 1969 and also took part in the Bentley Golden Jubilee 500 Mile Rally.

6½-Litre UL34

Chassis No: LB 2330   Engine No: KR 2695   Registered: March 1929

This Speed Six, now owned by Mr Bob May of Berkshire, England, has seen a varied life. Starting with a two-seater body by Barker & Co (Coachbuilders) Ltd, and engine No LB 2334 it had the registration number UL 20 and was owned by a Mr P.M. Stewart. It was rebuilt by Hofmann & Mountfort Ltd of Henley-on-Thames, who found that a new chassis frame was needed, and one was taken from a scrap car GF 6756 (Chassis SB 2771) and renumbered LB 2330. Since there was a change of chassis the registration authorities insisted that the car number should be changed to GF 6756. Before it actually bore this new number it was re-registered with the nearest possible number to the original and is now UL 34. When rebuilt it was fitted with a replica Vanden Plas four-seater tourer body. Since 1970 the car has done over 60,000 miles (96,540km) and has toured Australia, South Africa, USA, Canada, and most European countries. Flying Kilometre, Ghent, Belgium 1976 one way 102.459mph (164.857km/h).

Below: At the Welcombe Hotel, Stratford-upon-Avon, England in May 1968.

Facing page:

Top left: The start of a South African vintage car tour.

Top right: Rallying on the Cote d'Azur.

Upper middle: On an Alpine pass.

Lower middle: A halt on the La Clusaz-Antibes Rally.

Bottom right: UL 34 on wedding duty.

4½-Litre

Despite the satisfaction with which the 6½-litre was received, there was still a demand by Bentley enthusiasts for a more flexible and faster four-cylinder car, not to mention a certain Mr Foden (of steam-lorry fame) who said that he missed the 'bloody thump'! So a 4½-litre was built. The prototype, on a 10ft 10in (3.3m) chassis, was entered at Le Mans in 1927, together with two 3-litres which had run in the same race the previous year, and the new car proved to be very fast indeed, lapping early in the race at 72mph (115.84km/h). The team met near-disaster in the now famous 'White House' crash when the 4½ became too badly damaged to continue. However, the 4½'s showing in the race ensured production of the model, and deliveries started in late 1927.

The first standard 4½-litre cars used the 10ft 10in (3.302m) chassis of the 3-litre, with a radiator of the same shape but wider and with greater capacity and fitted with a thermostat in the water rail. The engine was based on the sound design of the 3-litre, but using a larger cylinder block, heavier crankshaft, 6½-litre con rods, and the sump of the later 3-litres. A C-Type gearbox was employed, using higher and closer ratio gears. Continued racing ensured that modifications were built into almost every series, (each series was made up of 25 cars). A new and now familiar 4½-type radiator with the lamp and trunnion brackets was fitted after about the first 100 cars were built. A Hardy Spicer propshaft, and a Bluemels spring spoke steering wheel, together with heavy type front axlebed and vertical SU, HVGS carburettors were other early changes.

Between 1927 and 1930, nine cars with a 9ft 9½in (2.98m) wheelbase were built. They were practically identical to the standard 4½ in every other respect, but were said to handle a little better, due to the reduced flexibility of the frame. The 4½ model

Below: 4½-litre chassis nearside.

Facing page:

Top and bottom: Probably more 4½-litre cars have been rebodied than any other model. SB 3535, which is owned by Mrs Nina Grieve of Scotland, is shown with original Charlesworth body, and as rebuilt by the late Mr James Grieve. (Chassis No AD 3658, engine No AD 3658).

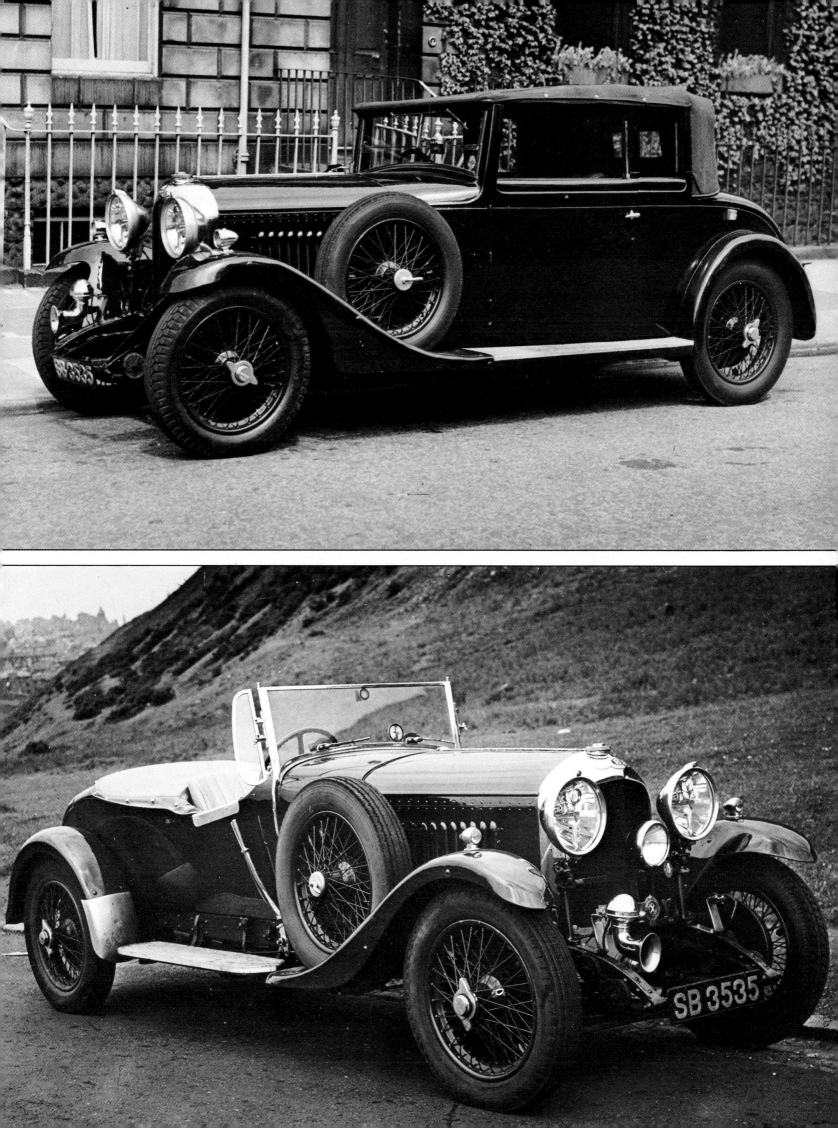

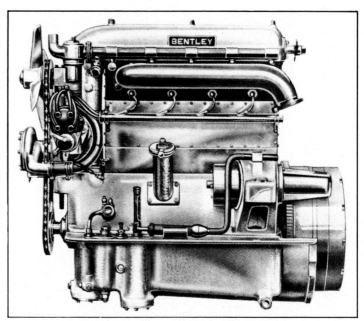

Above: Catalogue illustration of 4½-litre engine.

Top left: 4½-litre chassis offside.

Left: A sporting two-seater, price £1,380 in the 1928 catalogue.

Right: A sporting four-seater tourer, price £1,295 from the same catalogue.

achieved success at Le Mans in 1928, this time three 4½-litres forming the team, two of them new cars, and the third car the original one with its early distinctive radiator. Woolf Barnato and Bernard Rubin driving car No 4 won, covering 1,658.6 miles (2,653.83km) at 69.108mph (111.19km/h). The 4½-litre was proving popular and about 263 were built in the year.

The performance of the standard 4½-litre, when fitted with a Vanden Plas four-seater touring body, was excellent and in a road-test on 8 May 1928, *Motor* obtained a maximum speed of 90mph (144.8km/h) with a car which had the normal rear axle. During acceleration trials, 10 to 60mph (16.09 to 96.54km/h) in third gear was reached in 18 seconds, and maximum speed in the gears at 3,500rpm was 69mph (111.02km/h) in third, 56mph (90.10km/h) in second, and 34mph (54.70km/h) in first. It must be borne in mind that this was at a time when the legal speed limit was only 20mph! (32.18km/h).

In 1929, self-wrapping front brakes, plate clutch, a thicker chassis frame and direct metal con rods were fitted, and an Elektron bulkhead and components were used for the first time. Larger head lamps were also fitted. The extra power developed by the 4½ enabled coachbuilt saloon and drophead bodies to be carried reasonably satisfactorily, and many fine examples were fitted to the Bentley. A choice of axle and compression ratios was available to enable an owner to get the performance that he wished, be it acceleration or top speed.

In 1930, the heavy crankshaft and many standard components used in the supercharged engine were incorporated, the last twelve built (the XT series) also had the heavy crankcase and a front axle with integral jacking pad. Eventually deliveries to customers tailed off and finally registration of 4½s ended in September 1931.

However, we must also consider the six 4½-litre chassis (RC Series) that were built in 1936/7 to be 'W.O.' cars, as, like the 3-litre RC series, they were constructed from parts taken from the old company's parts stock, and put together by Bentley Motors (1931) Ltd. They incorporated parts of the late production cars, and most of them were fitted with fully-enclosed-style bodies, popular in the mid-thirties. Excluding the six RC chassis, 659 cars were built between 1927 and 1931, and for many Bentley enthusiasts there is nothing that gives such satisfaction as a four-cylinder 4½-litre tourer, with its long-legged gait, accompanied by that familiar burbling exhaust note and the whine of straight-cut gears.

SPECIFICATION

4½-LITRE

In production 1927-31.

Basic specification at introduction (with some later modifications):

ENGINE
4 cylinders; firing order 1, 3, 4, 2.

Bore	3.94in (100mm)
Stroke	5.51in (140mm)
Cubic capacity	4,398.24cc (268.3cu in)
Compression ratio	Very early models 4.8:1; saloons 5.1:1; open 5.3:1
Brake horsepower	Saloons 105; open 110
RAC rating	24.8hp

Valves and camshaft
Four tulip-shaped valves per cylinder operated by a single overhead gear-driven camshaft, operating forked double rockers to inlet valves and single rockers for exhaust valves.

Cylinder block
Cast-iron block and cylinder head (non-detachable) en bloc.

Crankcase and sump
Cast alloy crankcase and one-piece sump. Elektron on heavy crank engines.

Crankshaft
Light 47lb (21.15kg); heavy 72lb (32.4kg). Mounted in five white metal bearings. Con-rods with direct metal bearings, except later backed shell bearing to con-rods. Heavy crankshaft engines were fitted with Speed-Six con-rods.

Lubrication
Pressure feed to main bearings and big ends, splash to pistons and gudgeon pins. Sump capacity 20 pints (11.36 litres).

Ignition
Twin synchronised ML magnetos type ER4, two sparking plugs per cylinder, KLG483 or 1, Champion 16 or Lodge CV 18mm.

Carburettors
Two SU GS slopers; later two vertical HVGs SUs on common manifold.

Dynamo
Smith's type 2DA, with cutout. 12 volt system.

Starter
Smith's type 4LSA.

Instruments
Hobson petrol-level gauge, Jaeger speedometer, Smith switch and ammeter, oil gauge and, later models, eight-day bezel-wind Smith's clock.

Cooling system
Forced pump circulation gear driven from centre of cross-shaft. Capacity 46 pints (26.16 litres). Thermostat control. Four-bladed fan fitted to some cars and to those for overseas.

Petrol system
Autovac, 1 gallon (4.55 litres); tank 16 gallons (72.8 litres).

TRANSMISSION
Gearbox
Three-point suspension. C-Type for cars with heavy coachwork. D-Type for open cars.
  Oil capacity: 6 pints (3.41 litres).

Clutch
Inverted cone. Later cars (1929), single plate $10\frac{3}{4}$in (273mm) with Ferodo lining.

Propeller shaft
Open one-piece with plunging ('pot') joints. Later (1928), one-piece with Hardy Spicer joints, the hollow weldless tube acting as reservoir for the rear universal joint.

Rear axle and final drive
Semi-floating, spiral bevel (four-bevel pinion differential) giving engine to road wheel ratio in top of 15/53 (3.533:1).
  Oil capacity 3 pints (1.71 litres).

CHASSIS
Frame
Channel-section with four pressed-steel cross-members, gauge 0.156in (4mm). Later cars, 0.188in (5mm).

Suspension
Semi-elliptic springs front and rear (underslung) with gaiters.

Shock absorbers
Bentley & Draper Duplex or Hartford Duplex. Later cars, Bentley & Draper, single short arm type at front and size 4 at rear.

Brakes
Four-wheel with Bentley-Perrot shafts to front. Internal expanding. 16in (406mm) drums; Ferodo linings. Servo-type shoes on front from 1929; later cars had longer rear-brake shoes.

Front axle
'H'-section 40ton (40,640kg) tensile steel. Heavybed axle fitted

from chassis KM3092. Last seven cars had integral jacking pad.

Steering
Worm and wheel type; ratio 10.3:1.

Exhaust
A single exhaust manifold on near side to 'pepper pot' silencer to a single tailpipe on open cars. Double silencers for cars with closed coachwork.

Wheels
Rudge-Whitworth, well-base rim, detachable wire wheels, centre-locking with left- and right-hand threads.

Tyres
5.25in x 21in (133.35mm x 533.4mm) Dunlop.
5.25in x 31½in (133.35mm x 800.10mm) Goodrich.
5.25in x 32½in (133.35mm x 825mm) Goodrich.

PRINCIPAL CHASSIS DETAILS AND DIMENSIONS
Wheelbase: 9ft 9½in (2.98m), 15 only; 10ft 10in (3.3m).
Track: 4ft 8in (1.42m).
Overall length: Short 13ft 3in (4m); Long 14ft 4½in (4.38m).
Overall body width: 5ft 8½in (1.74m).
Turning circle: (Long chassis): Right 49ft (14.94m); Left 47ft (14.35m).
Ground clearance: 7¾in (197mm) with 32½in (825mm) tyres.
Weight (Long chassis): Chassis 25cwt (1,310kg).
With open body 32½cwt (1,638kg).
Performance (Long chassis):
  Maximum speed 92mph (147:2km/h) at 3,500rpm (10ft 10in wheelbase).
  Petrol consumption: 16mpg.
Price at introduction: Chassis (long) £1,050 plus £10 if modified to accept closed coachwork.
Complete car, open four-seater £1,295.
Number built: 665 (including 6 RC series).
Radiator badge: White enamel 'B' on black ground.

Two pictures of UC 1643, a recently re-bodied 4½-litre (Chassis No NT 3148, engine No NT 3148. Registered January 1928) now jointly owned by C.R. Dalton, D.W. Dalton, and F.E.W. Hine, who come from Hampshire, England. This car won the award for the best 4½-litre at the Bentley Drivers Club, Kensington Gardens, London, Concours in 1977. These pictures were taken at Oulton Park in May 1977.

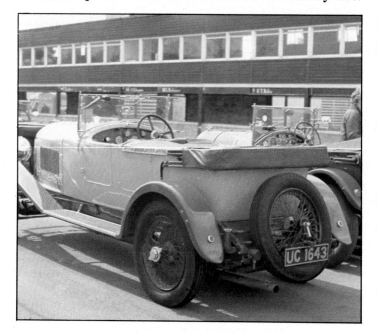

4½-Litre YW2557

Chassis No: KM 3088   **Engine No: MF 3175**   **Registered: June 1928**

YW 2557 is one of the cars that helped to create the Bentley legend. This car's first outing was in the Essex Car Club's Six Hour Race at Brooklands on 12 May 1928 (before registration), finishing in sixth place. The following month it was one of the works team of three cars in the Grand Prix d'Endurance at Le Mans, driven by F.C. Clement and Dr J.D. Benjafield, but retired when a cracked frame caused a broken pipe in the cooling system. The next season it was entered in the Double Twelve Hour Race at Brooklands in May, driven by S.C.H. Davis and Sir Ronald Gunter, and finished second at an average speed of 81.39mph (130.96km/h). In June 1929 it was again in the works team at Le Mans, and was the only car left with a 'bob-tail', the sister YV 7263 having been re-bodied with a 'Le Mans' type touring body. On this second outing, on the Sarthe Circuit she was driven by Dr J.D. Benjafield and Baron d'Erlanger and finished in third place, and Bentleys had achieved a Grand Slam with cars placed 1, 2, 3, and 4.

In 1930 YW 2557 was sold to a Mr Rose, whose family, apart from a short period, owned the car until his son sold it in 1971 to Mr W.D.S. Lake, who lives in Sussex, England.

Facing page:

Top left: The 'power house' of YW 2557.

Top right: Avro aircraft screens were fitted.

Bottom: The 'bob-tail'.

Below and following spread: YW 2557 at her present home.

4½-Litre UV6520

Chassis No: MF 3153   Engine No: KM 3905   Registered: August 1928

This car, delivered to the coachbuilders Vanden Plas (England) 1923 Ltd in May 1928, was first registered in August 1928, the first owner was Mr Gerald T.S. Bevan who kept the car for some time before selling it to an unknown second owner. The third owner was Lord Sempill, who bought UV 6520 in July 1938 and kept it until he sold it to Mr T.P. Breen, a keen Vintage Sports Car Club member, in July 1946. Mr Breen raced the car at VSCC meetings and hill climbs, and during his ownership it was re-painted from navy blue to British racing green.

In May 1965 it was acquired by Mr John Elvins of Worcester-shire, England, who takes it to club meetings, and keeps it within earshot of Shelsley Walsh. A very original car in superb condition.

Three pictures of UV 6520 when owned by Mr Breen:

Below left, centre: Racing at Silvester in 1949.

Below left, bottom: Anglo-American Vintage Car Rally at Prescott hill-climb 1954.

Facing page, top right: At home.

4½-Litre YW3774

Chassis No: 1192 (3-litre)   Engine No: UK 3298   Registered: 1928

YW 3774 is a car with a history. Generally known as EXP5 this car started life at Bentley Motors in 1928. At first sight this might be taken for a 3-litre with an original but not very smart Gurney Nutting four-seater touring body. On closer inspection it will be seen that although the radiator is similar to the 3-litre it has the greater height of the 4½-litre, and at the rear it will be noticed that the wings do not match – they have been like this as long as anyone can remember. As a result of Le Mans experience it was decided in 1928 to build the racing spares into a chassis rather than ship them across the Channel in crates. This spare car was used as a practice car for the team drivers and served as transport for the mechanics – if one of the team cars had trouble the spares were there. YW 3774 went with the Bentley team to Le Mans in 1928, 1929 and 1930. When the old firm was taken over in 1931 YW 3774 went to Rolls-Royce and was kept by them until sold to Flight Lieutenant McQueen in 1947. However, in order to save petrol during the war the original 4½-litre engine (EXP5) was replaced by a 3-litre engine (SE4). The car had various owners, and in April 1953 the present 4½-litre engine No UK 3298 (ex-chassis No AB 3354, registration No GU 252) was fitted. In 1968 it was acquired by Mr Michael Gillett. The car is now in the Fuad Majzub collection in Worcestershire, England.

Above right: Engine No UK 3298.

Below: The heightened 3-litre radiator.

Facing page, top right: The rear end of YW 3774 showing odd rear wings.

4½-Litre GU6544

Chassis No: AB 3373   **Engine No: AB 3374**   **Registered: May 1929**

This splendid two-seater drop-head coupé was built by Salmons & Son of Newport Pagnell, for a Mr E.W. Hunter, who must have been a keen sportsman because he had a special small door fitted behind the passenger door on the off side so that golf clubs, guns or fishing rods could be stowed with ease. This car is now owned by Mr George Milligen who lives in Norfolk, England.

4½-Litre SC7121

Chassis No:XF 3506   Engine No:XF 3503   Registered: April 1930

SC 7121 is probably the most original Vanden Plas four-seater Bentley in existence, and has had a very sheltered life. The first owner was a Miss L. Logan who only had it for a year before selling it to Mr G.H. Gregor, a Scotsman. In 1976 it was purchased from Mr Gregor by Mr R.A. Parker who lives in Warwickshire, England. It had covered only a little over 30,000 miles from new and still had the original works engine seals unbroken! It must also be one of the very few cars with the original cast exhaust fishtail with the name Bentley on it. Most of the paint work is original.

4½-Litre OV4754

One of the last twelve 4½-litre chassis to be built, this car is fitted with the heavy crankshaft engine which appeared as a result of the development work on the fifty supercharged cars built in 1930 and 1931. The substantial crankshaft and crankcase from what is virtually the blower engine without the supercharger produced a very strong unit and a final stage of 4½-litre engine development. The 10ft 10in chassis (3.3m) was originally fitted with an 'as new' Vanden Plas touring body by H.M. Bentley & Partners, and was owned briefly by Sir E. Bilsland of Glasgow, and in 1932 by Mr C. Kay of Solihull, Birmingham, England.

Late in 1932, Mr Henry Pursman purchased the car and owned it up to 1959, and during this twenty-seven years it travelled only 24,000 miles (38,616km).

However, in the mid-'thirties, Mr Pursman's family decided that a closed saloon of the streamlined style, then in fashion, was more desirable. So in 1936, Cooper Bodies of Putney Bridge Road, London, were commissioned to build a new sports saloon body. Cooper's had earlier purchased a streamlined body shell from Triumph Cars of Coventry, who before the war were well known for their own quality coach-built standard type bodies.

The chassis had covered less than 60,000 miles (96,540km) from new when it came into the possession of the present owner, Mr R.V. Roberts, with the engine still carrying lead seals to the sump!

4½-Litre DMX417

Chassis No: RC 42   Engine No: RC 491 E   Registered: 1936

DMX 417 is one of the six RC series 4½-litre cars built up from
spares by Rolls-Royce Limited in 1936, which was bodied by
Vanden Plas (England) 1923 Ltd of Hendon with a four-seater
drop-head body which has a wind-down hood. It was supplied
new to a Mr C.E. Wales, and is now part of the Fuad Majzub
collection in Worcestershire, England.

4½-Litre Pacey-Hassan

The Pacey-Hassan Brooklands track car was built in 1936 by Wally Hassan and Wally Saunders for E.W.W. Pacey using Bentley parts. The 1936 version had an unsupercharged 4½-litre engine bored out to 3.976in (101mm). Various compression ratios were tried and the most successful seemed to be 9:1. An exceptionally stiff chassis frame was built with Woodhead outrigged springs front and rear. A 1922 3-litre brakeless front axle was used with a 3.0:1 ratio back axle. This car was timed over the flying kilometre on the Railway Straight at Brooklands at 139.96mph (225.2km/h) and it raced four times at Brooklands during the 1936 season. Having suffered engine damage it raced in 1937 with a supercharged 3-litre engine but without success. In the immediate post-war years this car was owned by Geoffrey Kramer in two-seater road-going trim and covered many miles in competition and Continental touring. Today the car in 4½-litre unsupercharged form is part of the Fuad Majzub collection and has been driven in Bentley Drivers Club events at Silverstone during the last few years.

4½-Litre Supercharged

In 1928 H.R.S. 'Tim' Birkin (later Sir Henry), who was to become one of the most famous of the 'Bentley Boys', conceived the idea of supercharging a 4½-litre, with the blower fitted between the front dumb-irons and driven at engine speed by the crankshaft. 'W.O.' disapproved of this, but it had the approval of Woolf Barnato, who at this time was chairman and a major shareholder of the company. Tim Birkin obtained the backing of the Hon Dorothy Paget, a wealthy motor-racing enthusiast, to construct and race a team of 4½-litre supercharged cars and a works was set up at Welwyn in Hertfordshire, and a team of four cars was completed in 1929.

The basic design of the 4½ was adopted, and Charles Amherst Villiers drew out plans for a supercharger and designed a completely new crankshaft, rods, pistons, oil pump, etc, together with a new cylinder block. However, the dry sump lubrication that he specified was rejected by Birkin. The supercharger was a twin rotor, of Rootes principle, giving 10lbs per square inch (0.7kg per sq cm) at 25mph (40.22km/h) in top, but it did not exceed 11lbs per square inch (0.77kg per sq cm) at the highest engine speed. A 10ft 10in (3.302m) chassis was used, with a modified front cross-member and tie bar. Power was taken through a new strong D-Type gearbox, incorporating very close ratio gears, similar to the first A gearboxes. Despite the power absorbed by the supercharger, a considerable increase in bhp was achieved, in the region of 175 at the rear wheels, 45 more than the unblown 4½-litre Le Mans engine. Tim Birkin was determined to race the cars at Le Mans, but the supercharged cars did not compete in 1929, due to lubrication troubles.

After a lot of persuasion, Tim Birkin managed to convince Woolf Barnato that the supercharged 4½-litre should be entered by the works for Le Mans in 1930, and this meant that fifty cars had to be built in order to qualify for entry. The production cars were first shown at the Olympia Motor Show of 1929, and were on sale by April of 1930. A blower car driven by Tim Birkin and Jean Chassagne, car Number Nine, performed well in the race, setting up a lap time of 6min 48sec; 89.696mph (144.32km/h) on the 10.153 mile (16.33km) circuit with Birkin at the wheel – a time that was never beaten, but in the end proved too much for the tyres. Its shattering pace during the early part of the race, and the verve with which it was handled by Birkin, almost certainly helped beat off the Mercedes challenge. Few modifications were introduced during its short life, but in October 1930 Dorothy Paget withdrew her support from the Birkin stable, because of escalating costs and lack of success.

Despite achieving only a few outright successes, the supercharged car became the epitome of the full-blooded British sports car, with its suggestion of sheer power, induced by its superb lines and balance, an image it has never lost. The last of the fifty pro-

duction cars was delivered in September 1931. Subsequent to the works' withdrawal from racing, during a practice for the 1932 Easter meeting at Brooklands, Birkin in his track Bentley, with engine modifications including special con rods, larger Villiers blower boosting 12lbs per sq inch (0.83kg per sq cm) and with dry sump lubrication, raised the outer circuit record to 137.96mph (221.97km/h).

A Vic Berris drawing for 'Autocar'.

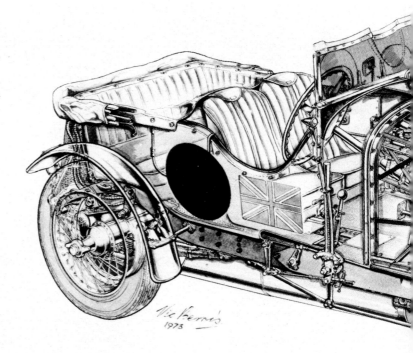

SPECIFICATION

4½-LITRE SUPERCHARGED

In production 1930-31 (Birkin cars 1929).

Basic specifications that differ from the standard unsupercharged 4½-litre car:

ENGINE

Compression ratio	4.5:1, very early cars
	5.1:1, standard
	5.3:1, later
Brake horsepower	175 at 3,500rpm with 9½lb (4.28kg) boost
	182 at 3,900rpm with 10lb (4.5kg) boost

Cylinder block
As 4½-litre, but with heavy foot.

Crankcase and sump
Very rigid cast Elektron with one-piece sump (later reinforced). Birkin cars only had large-capacity ribbed sump.

Crankshaft
Heavy type (counter balanced) mounted in five main bearings, caps reinforced with steel straps. Heavy two-bolt con-rods.

Lubrication
Supercharger fed from front of camcase, Birkin cars had 32 pint (18.2 litres) capacity.

Ignition
Twin Bosch FF4 or FU4B magnetos; two sparking plugs per cylinder, Lodge CV 18mm.

Carburettors
Two SU type HVGS, mounted on and feeding Amhurst Villiers Rootes type supercharger (two rotor). Drive to supercharger from front end of crankshaft through two Hardy Spicer joints to lower rotor.

Instruments
Smith thermometer, ammeter and bezel switch, boost gauges, speedometer, revolution counter, eight-day bezel-wind clock and Hobson petrol gauge, oil pressure gauge dial on instrument panel.

Cooling system
As standard 4½-litre, but 40 pint (22.75 litres) capacity.

Petrol system
Two auto-pulse electric pumps from 16 gallon (72.9 litres) tank; 25 gallon (113.8 litres) optional.

TRANSMISSION
Gearbox
D-type.

Clutch
Single plate, 12in (305mm).

Propeller shaft
Open one-piece shaft with Hardy Spicer joints; splined coupling on front joint.

Rear axle and final drive
Engine to road wheel ratio in top 13/46 (3.538:1) or 15/50 (3.3:1). A heavy 6½-litre axle nose-piece was fitted.

CHASSIS
Frame
As standard 4½-litre in 0.188in (5mm) gauge.

Suspension
Semi-elliptical springs, Woodhead on front and Berry on rear.

Shock absorbers
Bentley & Draper Duplex size 4 on front and rear.

Brakes
Front brake to four wheels, mechanical direct through compensating mechanism. Drums 15¾in (400mm), front servo type.

Steering
Ratio 10.25:1 or 11.0:1.

Tyres
6in x 21in (152mm x 533mm) Dunlop Reinforced medium pressure.

PRINCIPAL CHASSIS DETAILS AND DIMENSIONS
Overall length: 14ft 7in (4.45m).
Turning circle: Right, 49ft 6in (15.09m); Left 47ft 6in (14.33m).
Ground clearance: 8in (203mm).
Weight: Chassis 28½cwt (1,436kg).
       With open body 34cwt (1,714kg).
Performance: Maximum speed (*Motor* road-test April 1930).
       103mph (165.7km/h) at 3,500rpm.
       Petrol consumption 11mpg.
Price at introduction: Chassis £1,150.
       Complete car, open four-seater £1,395.
Number built: 50 (plus 5 Birkin cars).
Radiator badge: As standard 4½-litre.

4½-Litre Supercharged UU5871

Chassis No: HB 3402   Engine No: SM 3901   Registered: 1929

This car was the first of the supercharged 4½-litre Bentleys and was first raced by its owner H.R.S. (Tim – later Sir Henry) Birkin in the Six Hours Race at Brooklands in June 1929, but did not complete the race. It appeared again in the Irish Grand Prix at Phoenix Park, Dublin, two weeks later and was placed third with an average speed of 79mph (127.11km/h). It did not do so well in the Ulster TT when it was placed eleventh, and it caught fire and retired in the 500 Mile Race at Brooklands in October 1929. Up to this point the car had a Vanden Plas Le Mans type body, and had been driven by Tim Birkin. Twelve months later it again appeared in the October 500 Mile Race at Brooklands, but was fitted with a single-seater body and painted blue. Its next appearance in a major race was in October 1931, again in the 500 Mile Race at Brooklands, driven by Dr J.D. Benjafield, but it did not finish. The following year on the 24 March, with cylinder bore increased to 3.96in (100.5mm) and painted red, with Sir Henry Birkin driving, it broke the outer circuit track record at Brooklands with a speed of 137.96mph (221.976km/h) which remains unbroken.

The car is now owned by Mr B.M. Russ-Turner, who is the present Chairman of the Bentley Drivers Club, and is regularly driven at Vintage Sports-Car Club and Bentley Drivers Club Silverstone Meetings and at the Brighton Speed Trials. In 1976 it averaged 127mph (204.34km/h) over the two directions of the Flying Kilometre at Ghent.

Above right: UU 5871 racing at the Bentley Drivers Club meeting at Silverstone in 1977.

Below: The owner 'Rusty' Russ-Turner waiting to move out onto the starting grid at the Bentley Drivers Club Silverstone Meeting in 1973.

4½-Litre Supercharged UU44

Chassis No: HB 3416   Engine No: RT 7000   Registered: June 1929

This car was originally a standard 4½-litre with a Vanden Plas saloon body, which was used by the present owner Mr B.M. Russ-Turner as the basis for building a Brooklands replica with a two-seater body which had belonged to UU 5871. The super-charged engine was built from spares for 'Rusty' Russ-Turner's other car but many parts had to be specially made, which no doubt accounts for the engine bearing the number RT 7000. The car is regularly used in many vintage race and hill climb meetings.

4½-Litre Supercharged YU3250

Chassis No: HF 3187   Engine No: HF 3187   Registered: February 1928

Something of a mystery car, this. It would appear that this car, originally a standard 4½-litre with a Vanden Plas Le Mans sports body, was owned by Bernard Rubin (one of the 'Bentley Boys') and later sold to the Hon Dorothy Paget for converting to a supercharged competition car in 1929, and was raced in the 1929 Ulster TT and subsequently was entered for other events in 1929 and 1930, but never had much luck. While in Dorothy Paget's hands it had a new chassis which was given the number HB 3404 R, and the supercharged engine was No SM 3903. It would appear that the original chassis and engine when sold in 1930 to a Mr Anthony Bevan bore the original regstration YU 3250 and the supercharged

car when sold by Dorothy Paget in 1932 to a Mr C.J. Turner was re-registered as JH 3115. When this car was bought by the late Mr Harry Rose it was still JH 3115, but he was able to obtain the original registration number YU 3250 which had presumably become vacant. The car was raced by Harry Rose for many years and is now owned by his daughter, Mrs Ann Shoosmith, and is at the moment in the Castle Donnington Motor Museum, where it is on loan. The picture below was taken in September 1929. The others were taken at Bentley Drivers Club meetings at Silverstone in 1968 and 1972.

4½-Litre Supercharged GK3841

Chassis No: SM 3920   Engine No: SM 3924   Registered: November 1930

GK 3841 is one of the production run of fifty 'blown' 4½-litre Bentleys which had to be constructed in order that the Hon Dorothy Paget might enter a team for Le Mans. The car, fitted with a Vanden Plas four-seater touring body, was supplied to Mr R. Kershaw. For some years after the war it was owned by Mr R.A. Parker of Warwickshire, England, who eventually sold it to Mr Peter J. Sprague of Massachusetts, USA, who keeps the car in England. GK 3841 would appear to be in its original condition.

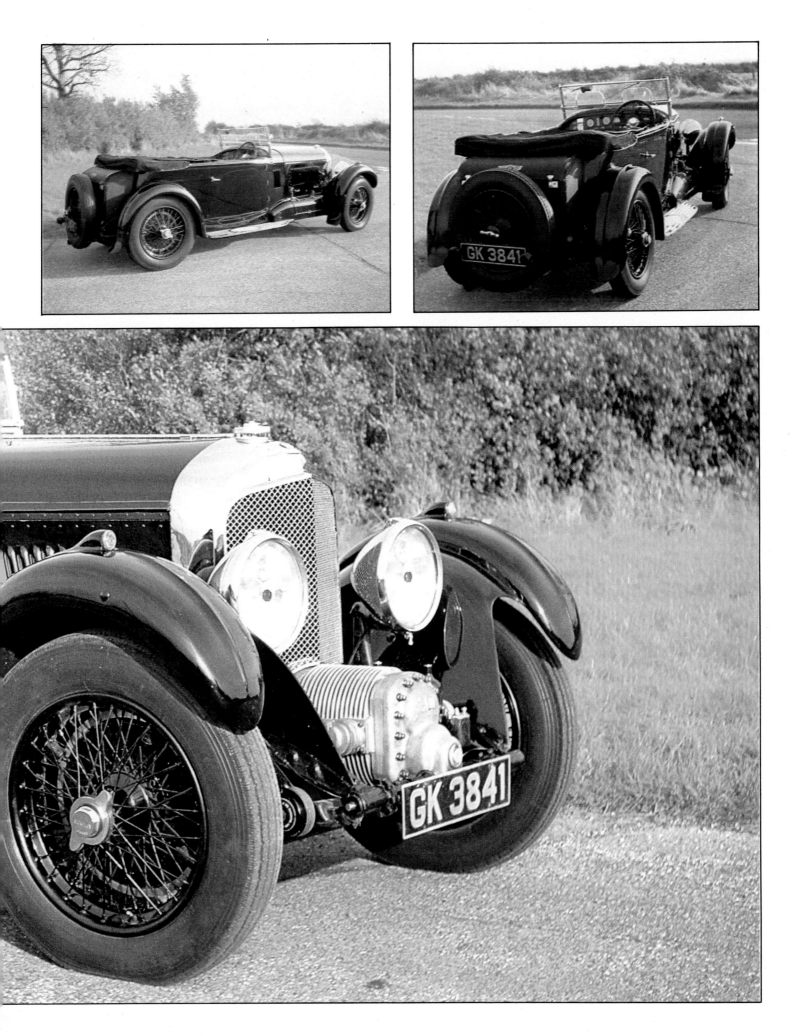

8-Litre

AN INTRODUCTION TO THE
8 LITRE BENTLEY

"**O**NE may discuss this or that point in the general detail or main design, attributing advantages to some things, and the inevitable disadvantages as well, but the real point that has made the Bentley car one of the most successful machines that has ever been built is simply that it is a Bentley; that despite all questions of design, the complete car has truly that mysterious quality which makes one forget it is a machine at all. To say that a car possesses that quality is to pay it the highest compliment in one's power."—*The Autocar, September 5th, 1930.*

In 1930, despite the shadow of financial difficulties that was again looming, W.O. Bentley introduced what was probably his finest car, the 8-litre, which was also the largest British car made. The engine of this vast motor car had a bore of 110mm (4.33in) with the same 140mm (5.51in) stroke of the 6½-litre, used the single inlet port block design, mounted on a stronger and thicker-walled but basically 6½-litre crankcase and sump. Two alternative compression ratios of 5:1 or 5.5:1, gave power outputs of 200bhp and 225bhp respectively. The rear of the camshaft was fitted with a Lanchester clutch-type damper similar to the later 6½-litre models, likewise the water-pump was driven from the front; the dynamo drive was again taken from the front of the crankshaft. The valve rockers

were adjusted through long detachable side plates in the main casing, which was fitted on top of the cylinder block.

Part of the inherent strength of a Bentley engine was the design feature by which the longbolts that secured the cylinder block to the crankcase also extended to the main bearing caps. This engine was constructed in the same manner. Compared to the engine layout of the 6½-litre, the cylinder block was turned round, putting the inlet manifold on the offside of the engine; this simplified the carburetter controls considerably. It was fitted via three rubber mountings into a deeper and stronger chassis having five tubular cross-members, and was offered with either a 12ft or the very long 13ft (3.66 or 3.96m) wheelbase. A three-point rubber-mounted F-Type gearbox was used which was an entirely new design; the case, split vertically, was fitted with twelve bearings and detached from the engine. Later a modified F gearbox was fitted which had an Elektron case, but both provided a gearbox of massive strength. The gear lever action was different, a much stronger movement

Above left: An 'Autocar' opinion reprinted in the 8-litre catalogue of 1930.

Below: GK 4300, chassis No YF 5008, engine No YF 5008, with Park Ward four-door saloon which was shown at the 1931 Motor Show at Olympia, London, and subsequently sold to a Mr R. Aldridge. The photograph was taken in December 1931.

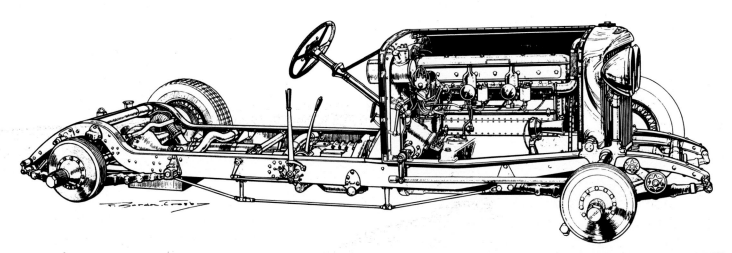

being involved between gears. Drive was taken by a Hypoid rear axle, to which larger wheel hubs were fitted, and the rear suspension was given more stability by setting the rear springs outside the main chassis-members. The brakes had two shoes to each rear drum instead of the usual four, and all four brakes were adjusted simultaneously by a wing-nut that projected through the frame near to the driver. In fact the construction of the car broke much new ground for the company. One other feature was the thermostatically controlled radiator shutters fitted to a new radiator shell, to which was bolted a separate radiator block.

The motoring press waxed lyrical about the car; it was described as 'unique, single in its kind of excellence', *Motor* 1930; 'One of the finest examples of British automobile engineering that has ever been produced', *The Sphere* 1931; 'No motor manufacturing company in the world has sprung into prominence so quickly as Bentley Motors Ltd, principally it is due to the fact that the car has always possessed such attractive lines, proved so reliable, and stood up to the roughest wear under the worst possible conditions', Captain Malcolm Campbell, *The Field* 1930. The *Autocar* of 5 December 1930, carried a road-test report on the car. 'Motoring in its very highest form: the tremendous performance', was the headline to the article. It commended the rigid chassis, which gave such a steady ride, but it considered the 'latent power' of the car to be its real strength: it was timed at 101.12mph (162.60km/h) over the measured ½-mile (805m), together with an effortless cruising speed of 70mph (112.63km/h). This same car was again tested by *Autocar* on the 4 April 1954, and it was still capable of 100mph (160.9km/h). Tremendous flexibility was embodied in the car, and even with heavy luxurious coachwork, and with a driver and three or more passengers, it still had genuine 100mph (160.9km/h) performance, with maximum bhp being developed at a little over 3,200rpm, it was also the first closed saloon car to lap Brooklands at over 100mph, a further example of the usable power it possessed.

One hundred chassis were built before the factory closed in 1931. Numbers were certainly restricted by the trade depression that existed at the time, but there was still a good market for the car. Manufacturing facilities at Bentley Motors were such that the chassis could be built at a cost of £935 and had it not been for the depression, the car might have sold well enough to make the company's future secure. A higher proportion of 8-litres has survived than almost any other model, a lasting tribute to the esteem in which it is held. Nearly one-third of the cars built were not completed with their bodies until 1932.

This magnificent and remarkably silent machine may well have directed the attention of the Rolls-Royce directors towards the receiver's sale of Bentley Motors Ltd as it certainly was in competition with their current Phantom II.

SPECIFICATION

8-LITRE

In production 1930-31.

Basic specification at introduction (with some later modifications):

ENGINE
6 cylinders; firing order 1, 4, 2, 6, 3, 5.

		With specialoid pistons
Bore	4.33in (110mm)	
Stroke	5.51in (140mm)	
Cubic capacity	7.983cc (487.14cu in)	
Compression ratio	5.1:1 or 5.5:1	5.3:1 or 6.1:1
Brake horsepower	200 or 225	225 or 230
RAC rating	44.9hp	

Valves and camshaft
Four tulip-shaped valves per cylinder operated by rear-driven single overhead camshaft in eight bearings to forked double rockers to inlet valves and single rockers to exhaust valves. A camshaft damper is fitted.

Cylinder block
Cast-iron block and cylinder head (non-detachable) en bloc with stainless-steel water-jacket plates.

Top: Gordon Crosby's drawing for the 'Autocar' of an 8-litre chassis.

Bottom: The 8-litre engine off side showing carburettors and Bosch magneto.

107

Crankcase and sump
Elektron cast crankcase and one-piece sump with flywheel cowl.

Crankshaft
Mounted in eight white metal bearings with front-mounted damper. Fully machined con-rods.

Lubrication
Pressure feed to main bearings, big ends and overhead gear. Splash to pistons and gudgeon pins. Sump capacity 40 pints (22.72 litres).

Ignition
Coil and Bosch magneto, FU6B, GF6A or SR6. Magneto fitted to off side. Two sparking plugs per cylinder, KLG1, Champion 16 or Lodge CV18mm. Magneto feeds the off side set and the coil the near side. The 12 volt coil is a Delco Remy MBS12.

Carburettors
Twin SU HO8 (2in) vertical square-throat fitted to off side of engine to a common manifold. Single diffuser device for slow running.

Dynamo
Smith's type 2.DAC3 or 2.DAC5 driven from the front of the crankshaft via two Hardy Spicer joints.

Starter
Bosch co-axial type BNE 2/12 RS2.

Instruments
Ignition testing switch AT speedometer and revolution counter, Smith's oil pressure gauge, Weston ammeter, Hobson petrol gauge and Jaeger eight-day clock.

Cooling system
Forced pump circulation and belt-driven fan with thermostatically controlled radiator shutters. Capacity 52 pints (29.6 litres).

Petrol system
Autovac, 1 gallon (4.55 litres); petrol tank 25 gallons (113.75 litres).

TRANSMISSION
Gearbox
Four forward speeds and reverse with right-hand gate change.
    F-Type gearbox: Ratios: Reverse, 2.926:1; First, 3.243:1; Second 1.792:1; Third 1.345:1; Top, direct.
(or modified F-Type with Elektron case, G-Type).
    Oil capacity: 9 pints (5.19 litres).

Clutch
Single dry plate, 14$\frac{1}{4}$in (362mm).

Propeller shaft
One-piece open shaft of weldless steel tube with two Hardy Spicer universal joints.

Rear axle and final drive
Semi-floating hypoid gears with four-bevel gear differential giving engine to road wheel ratios in top 15/53 (3.533:1); 14/57 (4.071:1); 16/53 (3.31:1) or 14/53 (3.785:1).
    Oil capacity 6 pints (3.41 litres).

CHASSIS
Frame
Deep channel-section with one pressed-steel cross-member and five tubular cross-members; 0.188in (5mm) gauge.

Suspension
Semi-elliptical front and rear with the rear springs outrigged.

Shock absorbers
Bentley-Draper Duplex, single short arm type at the front and Bentley-Draper hydraulic lever type at the rear. Tele-control shock absorbers often fitted as an extra.

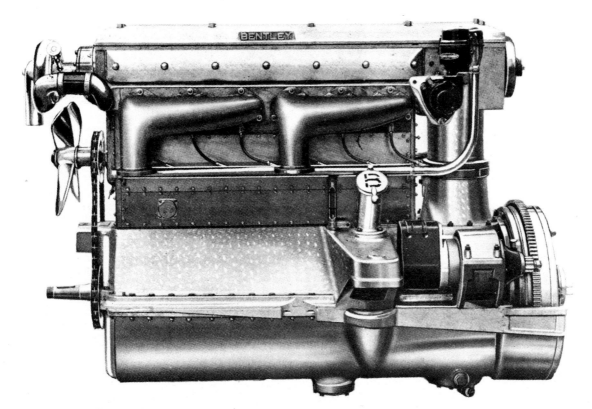

Top: The near side of the 8-litre engine showing exhaust manifolds and distributor for coil ignition system.

Above: An artist's impression from the 8-litre catalogue of Continental touring.

Facing page:

Top: Exotic coachwork. An illustration from the 1930 8-litre catalogue of a body design for a two-door close-coupled Weymann-type panelled saloon.

Lower: Method of gearbox mounting.

Brakes
Footbrake with Devandre vacuum servo assistance to four wheels with mechanical compensation. Handbrake to separate rear shoes. Front brakes, internal expanding self-wrapping.

Front axle
'H'-section 40 ton (40,640kg) tensile steel; heavy-type axle.

Steering
Worm and wheel (segment), ratio 13.75:1.

Lubrication
Tecalemit central control chassis lubrication.

Exhaust system
Twin exhaust manifolds with two exhaust pipes leading via a single pipe to a silencer and single tailpipe. A Continental exhaust cutout was available.

Wheels
Rudge-Whitworth, detachable wire, centre-locking with left- and right-hand threads. 3.15in (80mm) hubs were used.

Tyres
Goodrich standard 7in x 21in (178mm x 533mm).

Headlamps
Lucas P100 DB headlamps were standard.

PRINCIPAL CHASSIS DETAILS AND DIMENSIONS
Wheelbase: 12ft (3.66m) or 13ft (3.96m).
Track: 4ft 8in (1.42m).
Overall length: 16ft 9¼in (5.11m) or 17ft 9¼in (5.42m).
Overall body width: 5ft 9in (1.75m).
Turning circle: Right 53ft (16.15m) or 55ft (16.76m); Left 57ft 6in (17.53m) or 59ft 6in (18.14m).
Ground clearance: 7½in (190mm); low battery case.
Weight: Chassis 37cwt (1,865kg).
With open body 48cwt (2,419kg).
Performance: Maximum speed 104mph (167.3km/h).
Petrol consumption 11-12mpg.
Price at introduction: Chassis £1,850.
Number built: 100.
Radiator badge: Blue enamel background.

8-Litre MH1030

Chassis No: KL 3596   Engine No: BX 2424   Registered: 1924

MH 1030 is a car with a history and its life is best told by quoting from 'The How and Where of the 8-litre Bentleys' by Stanley Sedgwick.

'The Registration No MH 1030 has had an interesting history. It first appeared in 1924 on the "Sun" – the experimental 6-cylinder 4¼-litre Bentley which "W.O." took to Le Mans that year. Then it was on a Standard 6½-litre Vanden Plas tourer described in "Auto" of December 1925. It next appeared on the "Box", the Standard 6½-litre with a squarish saloon body, used by "W.O." for experimental work when developing the 8-litre. It was fitted with a bored-out 6½-litre engine and from time to time the chassis was strengthened to cope with the extra power.

'The Chassis No KL 3596 (a 4½-litre chassis number) appears in the car's registration book and on a plate riveted to the front cross-member – the original having been welded out of existence. In the absence of any reason for this "way out" chassis number, it seems just possible (if inexplicable) that the car acquired the chassis number of the 4½-litre to which the present body was originally fitted.

'This car passed from "W.O." to his brother "H.M." in the early '30s; "H.M." removed the saloon body and fitted an open Vanden Plas tourer from a 4½-litre. There seems no doubt that this car was the "Prototype 8-litre".

'What is open to question is how much, if any, of the original bored-out 6½-litre engine is still in the car. It seems that the engine, although now "back-to-front", has a "genuine" 8-litre block, but it is doubtful if anything of the experimental engine is still there, with the possible exception of the crankcase.'

Below: MH 1030 with 'Box' body photographed in November 1931 when in the hands of H.M. Bentley.

Right: MH 1030 as she is today in the ownership of Mr R.D. Weary of Florida, USA.

8-Litre GP401

Chassis No: YR 5095   **Engine No: YR 5095**   **Registered: June 1931**

GP 401 is an outstanding 8-litre which was supplied in June 1931 to Captain Woolf Barnato (chairman of Bentley Motors Limited) with a four-seater touring body built by Vanden Plas especially to the designs of its first owner. In 1932 it was sold by the Bentley Company to Flight Lieutenant Reggie Presland (now Wing-

Commander retired).

Today, the car is completely original and unmodified. The pillar-swivel spotlight and horn are of French manufacture and fitted for Barnato when new – no doubt fitments he had seen on one of his many trips to the French Riviera. One peculiarity is that all plated

trims are made of copper – a special request of Barnato – and as good today as when they were made.

Wing-Commander Presland keeps the car in regular use and, except during five years of war, has always had it available. Now, because of the price of petrol, it does not get used as much as the owner would like. The car has special air cushions for the front seats which need re-inflating from time to time, so a bicycle pump is carried amongst the tools! It is interesting to find that on the underside of the timber frame of the front seats the word BARN-ATO is written in chalk – no doubt put on when the car was being serviced at Cricklewood in 1931.

On taking delivery of the car in 1931 Woolf Barnato took it to America for his honeymoon with his second wife, and motored some thousands of miles on transcontinental roads.

8-Litre GK706

Chassis No: YF 5002   **Engine No: YF 5002**   **Registered: November 1930**

GK 706 was the second in the series of a hundred 8-litres and registered in the name of W.O. Bentley, and was used as his personal transport until the liquidation. The car has since had six further owners before joining the Fuad Majzub collection in Worcestershire. As can be seen from the photographs, the car is fitted with a rather narrow panelled Weymann saloon which was built by H.J. Mulliner & Co Ltd, of Chiswick, London.

GK 706 has been featured in many books and magazine articles. On his eightieth birthday in 1968, W.O. Bentley was entertained to lunch by members of the Bentley Drivers Club and GK 706 was used to take him to the function.

114

8-Litre UL7

Chassis No: YM 5050   Engine No: YR 5084   Registered: April 1932

UL 7, starting life as VC 9, was first owned by a Mr S.H. Row-botham and it was fitted with a Sedanca de Ville body by Arthur Mulliner of Northampton on the 13ft (3.96m) chassis. In 1936 the third owner, Mrs N.V. Flemmich, had the body removed, the chassis shortened to 12ft (3.66m) and had a new Sedanca de Ville body built for it by Barker & Co (Coachbuilders) of London, but only kept the car for a short while before selling it to a Mr A.C. Clark who decided to dispose of the Barker body, lower the radiator and scuttle by 5in (127mm) and have a four-seater sports body built by Corsica Coachworks of Cricklewood, London. At this time a third SU carburettor was fitted, the compression ratio was raised to 6:1 and back axle ratio altered from 3.7 to 3.3:1.

After another twenty-five years and two more owners it became the property of Mr Stanley Sedgwick – President of the Bentley Drivers Club – and has accomplished many outstanding trips since, one of the most noteworthy being 1,000 miles (1,609km) in one day on English roads which was accomplished on 20 June 1972. In fact, 1,000.5 miles (1,609.8km) were completed in an overall time of 17 hours and 37 minutes – a total driving time of 15 hours 25 minutes which gave an average speed for the 1,000 miles (1,609km) of 64.8mph (104.24km/h); petrol consumption was 10.2 miles per gallon. A valiant effort by both driver and car.

The photographs of UL 7 were taken at the Bentley Drivers Club Rally at Kensington Gardens, London, in 1977.

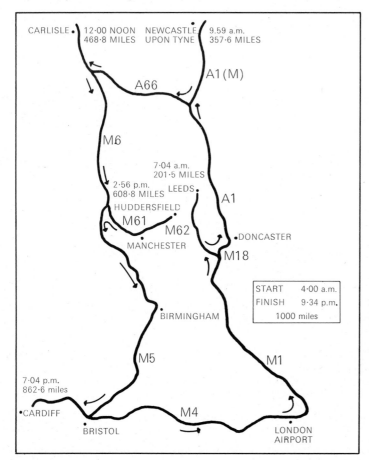

CARLISLE • 12·00 NOON 468·8 MILES   NEWCASTLE UPON TYNE   9.59 a.m. 357·6 MILES

A66   A1(M)

M6

7·04 a.m. 201·5 MILES

2·56 p.m. 608·8 MILES   LEEDS

HUDDERSFIELD   A1

M61   M62   • DONCASTER

MANCHESTER   M18

START	4·00 a.m.
FINISH	9·34 p.m.
	1000 miles

BIRMINGHAM

M5   M1

7·04 p.m. 862·6 miles

• CARDIFF   M4

BRISTOL   LONDON AIRPORT

8-Litre GX8867

Captain G.C. Blundell, then a junior officer in the Royal Navy, had his first Bentley in the 1930s. As one would expect, this was an open 3-litre, but it was sold when his duties took him overseas. When Captain Blundell retired from the Royal Navy in 1957 he decided that another Bentley was the car to have, and after much searching acquired an 8-litre GX 8867 from Alick Pitts, a Bentley enthusiast who owned a garage in Solihull, England.

GX 8867 was first registered in June 1932. It has a 12ft (3.656m) chassis and would appear to have been the next to last 8-litre Bentley constructed. This car has a two-door coupé body built by the Mayfair Carriage Co Ltd, of West Kilburn, London, and it was supplied new to a Mr C.G. Heywood, who had the car for only a short while and sold it to Mr H.J. Thomas, who was a director of the Bristol Aeroplane Company. While in his ownership the 21in (533mm) wheels were replaced by 19in (483mm), the mudguards altered and new running boards fitted that incorporated tool boxes. This work was done for Mr Thomas by 'Sajito'. The car was off the road from 1940 to 1948 and stored in the Bristol area. When retaxed in 1948 it was in the name of A.W. Waterman, who, the next year sold it to Mr C.R. Townsend, of Solihull. Mr Townsend also owned another 8-litre at the same time. When he died in 1958 both cars passed through the hands of Alick Pitts for resale.

Since the car has been in the hands of Captain Blundell it has been restored to its original condition with new wings and running boards and again has 21in wheels. At some time during its life the headlamp posts have been shortened, thus lowering the lamps. GX 8867 has covered approximately 249,000 miles (400,890km) since new and is regularly to be seen at Bentley Drivers Club meetings.

Left: In 1934, before alteration to running board and wings.

Below: Leaving a stately home (that Captain Blundell says is not his!).

Facing page:

Top: In 1953 after alteration.

Bottom: Original wing line and running board restored.

Following spread: The grandeur of an 8-litre.

4-Litre

The last model to be built by the old company, was the 4-litre. This 3,915cc 6-cylinder car was built at the insistence of the board to compete directly with the 20/25 Rolls-Royce, but 'W.O.' was not happy with it, for it had neither the acceleration nor the speed that people had come to expect from the Bentley marque, and in this respect it was not a success.

The engine was of Ricardo design, with push-rod operation of overhead inlet valves and side exhaust valves, thus differing from any previous Bentley engine made. Elektron was used for the crankcase and sump, with a cast-iron cylinder block and detachable cylinder head. An extremely rigid crankshaft was installed, carried by seven main bearings. Ignition was by coil only. The engine was mounted on longitudinal tubes, attached to the chassis by rubber anchorages. The double-drop chassis frame, with seven tubular cross-members, and the modified F-Type gearbox, were very

similar to those of the 8-litre, although the final drive was through a spiral bevel rear axle similar to that of the 6½-litre car. The chassis was fitted with Tecalemit chassis lubrication, operated by a central lubricator mounted on the dashboard. Long semi-elliptic road springs were used, those at the front shackled at the rear, unlike the 8-litre. A new type of steering box was constructed, with a worm and wheel mechanism. The braking system was an entirely direct mechanical operation, no servo being employed, and departed from previous practice in that the rear brakes were actuated by cables instead of the usual rods.

The first car was registered in May, 1931, but only 50 chassis

Below: Two catalogue illustrations of suggested coachwork for the 4-litre Bentley which probably never materialised.

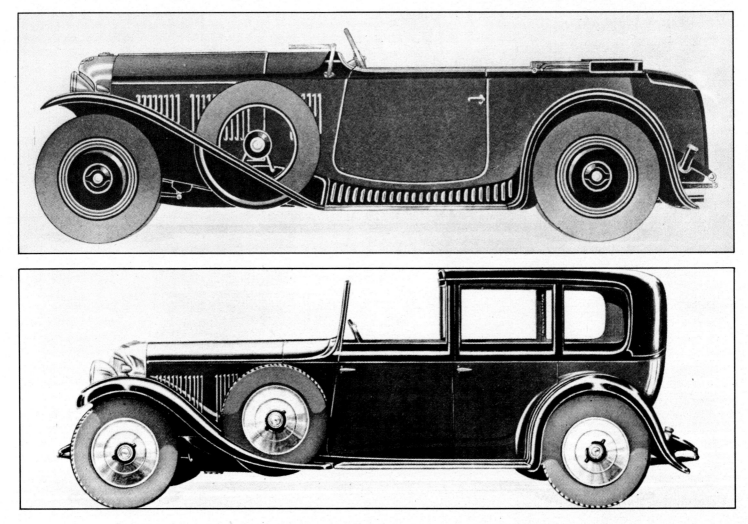

were built before the liquidation, 39 of them the short 11ft 2in (3.40m) wheelbase model, the others having an 11ft 8in (3.556m) wheelbase. However, the last car was not registered until June of 1933, and was possibly one of the chassis bought by Jack Barclay Ltd, after production had ceased. More than 33 saloons were built on the 50 chassis produced, suggesting that the 4-litre was more suited to this type of body than the open ones built in profusion on the previously constructed high performance 4½- and 6½-litre chassis.

SPECIFICATION

4-LITRE

In production 1931 only.

Basic specification at introduction (with some later modifications):

ENGINE
6 cylinders; firing order 1, 4, 2, 6, 3, 5.

Bore	3.35in (85mm)
Stroke	4.52in (115mm)
Cubic capacity	3,915cc (239cu in)
Compression ratio	5.5:1
Brake horsepower	120 at 4,000rpm
RAC rating	26.8hp

Valves and camshaft
Two valves per cylinder. Overhead inlet valves in cylinder head and side exhaust valves push-rod operated. Both sets of valves were adjusted from side camshaft cover plate.

Cylinder block
Cast-iron mono block with detachable cast-iron cylinder head. BHB pistons. Later, sloped and inverted Vee pistons were used.

Crankcase and sump
Elektron alloy crankcase and separate cast Elektron sump.

Crankshaft
Mounted in seven white metal bearings.

Lubrication
Pressure fed to main bearings, big end and overhead valve rockers. Sump capacity 24 pints (13.65 litres).

Ignition
Bosch coils, 12 volt, with spare coil fitted, via distributor to one sparking plug per cylinder, Lodge CV or Champion 7 18mm. Automatic and hand control of ignition.

Carburettors
Twin SU HV5 fitted to off side of engine on common manifold with auxiliary slow-running carburettor.

Top: Max Millar's cut-away drawing of a 4-litre chassis for the 'Autocar'.

Bottom: A painting by Le Breton reproduced from the 4-litre catalogue.

Dynamo
Smith's constant voltage, 12 volt.

Starter
Bosch, CV type mounted on off side of engine fitted with slow speed pinion engagement.

Instruments
AT speedometer, clock, oil pressure gauge, Hobson petrol gauge, water temperature gauge.

Cooling system
Centrifugal water-pump driven in tandem from dynamo and belt-driven fan. Radiator shutters operated by Smith's thermostat. Capacity 48 pints (27.3 litres).

Petrol system
Autovac, 1 gallon (4.5 litres); petrol tank 20 gallons (91 litres).

TRANSMISSION
Gearbox
F-Type or modified F (G-Type).

Clutch
Single dry plate.

Propeller shaft
Open single-piece with Hardy Spicer universal joints.

Rear axle and final drive
Semi-floating spiral bevel with four-bevel differential giving engine

to road wheel ratios in top 11/57 (5.18:1), 12/55 (4.58:1) or 12/57 (1.75:1).

Oil capacity 5 pints (2.84 litres).

CHASSIS

Frame
Very strong deep 'U'-section with seven large-diameter tubular cross-members, double drop design; 0.188in (5mm) gauge.

Suspension
Semi-elliptical front and rear fitted with gaiters.

Shock absorbers
Bentley-Draper Duplex, single short-arm type at front, Bentley-Draper double-acting hydraulic type (H Model) on rear.

Brakes
Four-wheel internal expanding type operated mechanically and direct through compensating mechanism, self-servo type front. Two shoes on each of the four wheels. Handbrake on rear only via separate cable control. Ferodo linings were used.

Front axle
'H'-section high-tensile steel.

Steering
Worm and wheel type; ratio 12.0:1.

Lubrication
Tecalemit central control chassis lubricator.

Exhaust system
Single-piece exhaust manifold fitted to near side of engine to single silencer and tailpipe.

Wheels
Rudge-Whitworth detachable wire with well-base rims. Centre locking with left- and right-hand threads.

Tyres
Goodrich standard 6.50in x 20in (165mm x 508mm).

Headlamps
Bosch.

PRINCIPAL CHASSIS DETAILS AND DIMENSIONS
Wheelbase: 11ft 2in (3.4m) or 11ft 8in (3.56m).
Track: 4ft 8in (1.42m).
Overall length: 15ft 10¾in (4.85m) or 16ft 8in (5.08m).
Overall body width: 5ft 8½in (1.74m).
Turning circle: Right 47ft (14.33m); Left 46ft (14.02m).
Ground clearance: 7in (178mm).
Weight: Chassis 32½cwt (1,638kg).
        With open body 39cwt (1,966kg).
Performance: Speed in excess of 80mph (128.7km/h).
        Petrol consumption 14-15mpg
Price at introduction: Chassis £1,225. Complete car £1,860.
Number built: 50.
Radiator badge: Blue enamel background.

Left: One of the few 4-litres still left, seen at Oulton Park, England in 1977.

Below: Radiator badge.

4-Litre GW 7429

Chassis No: VA 4088   **Engine No: FF 4022**   **Registered: March 1932**

GW 7429 must be the only technically one-owner vintage Bentley in existence. Purchased new by the late Mr S.S. Lewis, the car is now owned by his daughter, Miss Elizabeth Lewis, who lives in Gloucestershire, England. The car, in original condition with a four-door saloon body by Thrupp & Maberly Ltd of London, is still regularly used and attends most Bentley Drivers Club activities in the area in which the owner lives. It carries one of the much-sought-after winged 'B's on the radiator cap, shown in the picture opposite.

4-Litre ALC250

Chassis No: VA 4100   Engine No: VP 4028   Registered: June 1933

ALC 250 was the last 4-litre chassis built, and probably the last car built by the old company, and was no doubt one of those bought by Jack Barclay Ltd who had the drop-head coupé body built for it by Freestone & Webb Ltd of Willesden, London. The first owner was a Mr H. Wincott. At the time the photographs were taken the car was owned by Mr J.H. Brooks of Clwyd, Wales, who has since sold it. In the photographs of the engine it is interesting to note the stove-enamelled exhaust manifold which was a feature of some 4-litre cars.

Following spread: ALC 250 again.

Take-over

At the end of 1929, despite successes on the track, and a splendid range of models, the problem of finance was again rearing its head, and became acute in 1930. The Wall Street crash of 1929 and the dramatic fall of the stock market that followed, heralded the imminent slump. The effect of these conditions on the company was only delayed by the success that the 8-litre achieved at the 1930 Olympia Motor Show. Despite an intensive sales drive by Hugh Kevill-Davies, who had recently returned to the company as sales manager, heading a demonstration team on a tour of the country, meeting agents and customers alike, general sales continued to decline. Mr Montgomerie, who was company secretary, wrote to Rolls-Royce discussing the possibilities of a merger, but according to information available, nothing conclusive appears to have happened.

The need to build 50 Blower $4\frac{1}{2}$s to comply with Le Mans entry regulations had not helped matters. It was an expensive exercise, with no long production run to recover costs, and resources were further taxed by pre-production demands of the 4-litre. Had the plan to go public, which had been discussed for some twelve months or more, gone ahead, and had production been concentrated on fewer models, including the more profitable 8-litre, then the company might have survived, as by now, for the first time, it had the tremendous benefit of its own machine shop at Cricklewood.

In 1931 the financial situation rapidly became critical. Captain Woolf Barnato, who was still chairman and one of the main shareholders, was in America on personal business, and it seems he decided not to repay sums of £25,000 and £40,000 due under two mortgages. The company had already been through three financial restructuring operations during its ten-year life, and this last problem was the final straw. Stocks had been building up and on 18 June 1931 they included 53 8-litre chassis (including three consigned to French coachbuilders and four company cars) and 32 4-litre chassis which included four company cars. On 10 July 1931, Mr J.K.

The Oxgate Lane frontage of the Cricklewood factory photographed in June 1932.

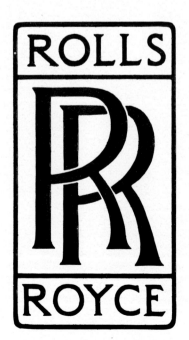

132

Carruth was appointed receiver by Woolf Barnato, and the London Life Association, another major shareholder, followed four days later with the appointment of Mr P.R. Frere to act in a similar capacity. On 10 September 1931 the company was voluntarily wound up under the liquidator, Mr Robert Montgomerie.

'W.O.' had been negotiating with D. Napier and Son of Acton during the period of liquidation and winding up, with the intention of moving to Napier's to design a car for them. Napier had the highest esteem for the Bentley name and design team, and they were quite prepared to take over the company. The car was to be called a Napier-Bentley and was to be of 6½-litre capacity, encompassing all the attributes of the 8-litre, but to be of lighter weight and reduced proportions, fitted into a lower sporting chassis. However, it was not to be; during an extraordinary court session, when the Napier offer, which had been accepted, was to be agreed formally by the judge, the proceedings were interrupted by someone who was said to be acting on behalf of the British Central Equitable Trust, with a bid slightly higher than that made by Napier's. After each side had retired to consider their positions, a further 'sealed offer' bid was submitted by each party, and the next day it was announced that 'the Syndicate' had won the day, though it seemed to be only a matter of a few hundred pounds. It was not clear who was behind the Syndicate, but subsequently it was revealed that the company that had mounted the successful bid was Rolls-Royce.

W.O. Bentley very shortly moved over to the Rolls-Royce showrooms at 14/15 Conduit Street, to work with Mr P. Northey on technical liaison, and after a period looking after the London demonstration cars, he became responsible for extensive road testing of the Rolls-Royce cars, and later the new Bentley 3½-litre. So the end of an era was reached, certainly with regard to the type of car built by the old company, and in terms of design of the Bentley Motor Car, for 'W.O.' was never again to design for the Bentley name.

Some 140 more or less completed chassis were bought from Bentley Motors (1931) Ltd, (the name of the new company) by Jack Barclay. These were completed and sold over the next two years, helping to bridge a gap left by the collapse of the old company, until the products of the new organisation were available. Several times in a letter written in June 1930 to Rolls-Royce by J.K. Carruth, who was Managing Director of Bentley Motors Ltd, he mentions 'the new 8½-litre'; whether or not this was a typing error has not been established. A further point of interest is that it is clear from correspondence that certain approaches had been made to Rolls-Royce by J.K. Carruth and not by 'W.O.' It would seem that two entirely different courses of action were being considered at the time of the final financial crisis. Records show that Rolls-Royce paid the Receiver £125,275 for the assets of Bentley Motors Limited.

3½-Litre

The Bentley Company and assets purchased by Rolls-Royce in 1931, were re-formed as Bentley Motors (1931) Ltd, operating from showrooms retained at 16 Conduit Street, London W1, over which were the offices where the original 3-litre was designed. The showrooms had been those of the London agents for the old Bentley Company. (As a matter of interest, the Rolls-Royce showrooms were on the opposite corner, at 14/15 Conduit Street.) It was almost another two years, however, before the first car from the new company was announced, and it was created without 'W.O.' being involved in its design, although he was responsible for some road-test work in his position as technical adviser to the Managing Director. Mr E.W. Hives (later Lord Hives), together with Mr Roy Robotham, certainly inspired the design and gave final impetus to a decision on form, and eventually to production. Sir Henry Royce died on 22 April 1933, and whilst he did not see the fruition of their labours, he definitely played a part in the development of the car.

In the autumn of 1933, the first of the new generation of cars appeared, the 3½-litre. It was born out of development work that had been carried out on a prototype Rolls-Royce, code-named the

A 3½-litre Bentley chassis being built alongside Rolls-Royces at Derby.

'Peregrine', which never reached production. It had been designed as a fast light-weight, economical car, able to meet the challenge of the depression, which had seen the fall in demand for large 6- and 8-litre cars such as the 40/50 Rolls-Royce, Mercedes, Hispano-Suiza or Isotta Fraschini. The depression had considerably reduced the number of surviving manufacturers.

The new Bentley which was built in the Rolls-Royce works at Derby had a prototype chassis, but it was fitted with a more powerful tuned twin-carburettor version of the Rolls-Royce 25/30hp engine using a different cylinder head, camshaft and with a higher compression ratio. It was launched with the now familiar phrase, 'The Silent Sports Car'. The chassis price was £1,100 and it carried a three year warranty; the factory cost was calculated to be in the region of £678.

A total of 1,177 3½-litre Derby cars were constructed and various bodies were available from the established coachbuilders of the day, but during the period from 1933 up to the war, the number of coachbuilders in business was continually diminishing. Bentley Motors (1931) Ltd produced only the chassis, and Park Ward were entrusted with the lion's share of the coachwork, building no less than 1,059 bodies, out of a total of 2,411 constructed on both the 3½ and 4¼ chassis. A large number of Park Ward steel bodies were built with their special all-steel framework, protected by Patent Number 470698; five others, Thrupp and Maberly, Vanden Plas, H.J. Mulliner, Hooper, and Gurney Nutting furnished another 776 cars. Vanden Plas in particular made some wonderful two-seater open bodies. Forty-one other coachbuilders equipped the further 576 with individual designs to special order. The Derby chassis seemed to lend itself to the sleek elegant bodywork that was the fashion, and the thirties probably saw coachwork at the height of its achievement.

The claims by its makers that 'this car, of moderate size could carry four people in comfort at a high average speed, able to perform under all conditions with performance and peace', was quoted in their sales brochure, without any fear of contradiction.

The six-cylinder engine of 3,669cc capacity, 6.5:1 compression ratio, with push-rod overhead valves, two per cylinder in a detachable cast-iron head, had a crankshaft carried in seven main bearings, and was fitted with a patent clutch type vibration damper; coil ignition was employed. The engine and gearbox were in one unit, and were mounted at the front end on a pivoted twin-tube bearer, in a chassis of conventional design, virtually identical to the prototype, but with a fully-floating hypoid-type axle. This was the first Bentley to have syncromesh gears, although only on third and top. The brakes used a friction disc clutch servo, driven from the gearbox, and were efficient and excellent in their operation.

Early models of the car were prone to front-end stability problems, and modifications included an extra front-chassis cross-member and an unusual harmonic stabilising front bumper! Towards the end of 1934 a hand-operated rear shock-absorber ride control was introduced. All the cars had central-control chassis lubrication and 18in (457mm) wheels on a wheelbase of 10ft 6in (3.2m). When numbering the chassis, 13 was omitted, and was never used in the future, even up to and including the post-war cars. An interesting device was fitted to some cars, consisting of a lever operating a flap on the exhaust immediately behind the first expansion box, so cutting out the further silencing equipment and giving slightly increased performance. This was known as the Continental Touring Device. A similar contraption was used in the 1930s by Captain Barnato on his 1931 8-litre, YR 5095. Not everyone it seemed wanted to motor in silence, the healthy roar of

A Derby-built 3½-litre chassis B112CR engine P4BM registration number FP 1111, now the property of Mr J.R. Beckingham of Lincolnshire, England.

an exhaust being quite acceptable and even desirable to some enthusiasts.

On 18 May 1934 *Autocar* reported on a road-tested Park Ward saloon, and recorded a best speed of 92.24mph (148.41km/h), and 0 to 50mph (0 to 80.45km/h) through the gears in 13.4 secs. The outstanding stamina and durability that these cars possessed attracted many famous sporting drivers in the mid-thirties, who used their 'Derby' cars for pre-race practising. Amongst them were Raymond Mays, George Eyston and E.R. (Eddie) Hall.

The Bentley marque had a brief association with racing again in 1934, when Eddie Hall, an enthusiastic Bentley owner and driver, having used a 3½ for initial practice over the Mille Miglia course, was so impressed with its performance, that he asked Rolls-Royce if he could enter a car in the Ulster TT, run on the Ards circuit outside Belfast. It was fitted with a special four-seater body by Offord, and certain engine tuning carried out which included raising the compression ratio to 7.75:1 and the fitting of larger inlet valves resulted in the engine giving approximately 163bhp. The car was entered privately by E.R. Hall, and some of the preparatory work was carried out by the factory. He finished second in this race at a speed of 78.40mph (126.16km/h) which was the fastest average speed and he also made the fastest lap at 81.15mph (130.57km/h). He again finished second in 1935 with an average speed of 80.36mph (129.30km/h). To have obtained works backing, even in a limited way, was a real achievement, the magnitude of which can be judged by the fact that the last time Rolls-Royce had supported racing activity was when they competed in the Alpine trial of 1913. There is no record that they have ever become involved since, although consideration was probably given to Le Mans, just prior to the Second World War.

In 1936, the car was fitted with the later 4¼-litre engine probably giving 170bhp, and a modified two-seater body, and Hall again took second place at Ards with a speed of 80.81mph (130km/h). However, he was never quite able to beat the handicapper. The car also made several appearances at the Shelsley Walsh Hill Climb. After the war the car raced at Le Mans, where, in 1950, it performed very creditably, finishing eighth at 82.95mph (133.47km/h) for the twenty-four hours, driven by E.R. Hall and T. Clarke. It is now in the Briggs Cunningham collection in the United States.

135

SPECIFICATION

3½-LITRE

In production 1933-36.

Basic specification at introduction (with some production modifications):

ENGINE

Four-point mounting with torsion flexibility.
6 cylinders; firing order 1, 4, 2, 6, 3, 5.

Bore	3¼in (82.5mm)
Stroke	4½in (114mm)
Cubic capacity	3,669cc (223.9cu in)
Compression ratio	6.5:1
Brake horsepower	110/120 (approximate)
RAC rating	25.3hp

Valves and camshaft

Two valves per cylinder, overhead, operated by push-rods and rockers from camshaft situated in the crankcase, driven by helical gears and carried in seven plain bearings.

Cylinder block and pistons

Monobloc cast-iron with detachable cast-iron head. Split skirt pistons; Aerolite on later cars.

Crankcase and sump

Aluminium crankcase and sump, cast in two pieces.

Crankshaft

Mounted in seven white metal lined bearings supported in the top half of the case. Vibration damper fitted at the front end.

Lubrication

Pressure fed to crankshaft bearings, gudgeon pins and valve rockers, circulating through a sump filter. Sump capacity 14 pints (7.96 litres).

Works official photographs of the 3½-litre engine. In the upper picture the ignition coils are not shown, and in the lower one there is no cap to the sump filler-pipe.

Below: A Gordon Crosby chassis drawing of the 3½-litre for the 'Autocar'.

136

One of the many very attractive bodies built on the 3½-litre chassis.

Ignition

By coil of Rolls-Royce manufacture, rated at 8 volt approximately, and ballast resistance. Automatic advance and retard control by centrifugal governor in distributor to one sparking plug per cylinder, KLG FLB30X or Champion LB8 14mm. Spare coil fitted. Over-riding ignition hand control on steering column.

Carburettors

Twin 1⅜in (38mm) SUs (HV3 type) with water-heated induction manifold fitted to off side of engine. Mixture control from cold start operated by hand control on steering column.

Dynamo

Positive drive at engine speed from camshaft gear. Two brush, automatic regulator type B2 CJ 1, dynamo of Rolls-Royce manufacture to 1 x 12 volt 50 amp hour battery.

Starter

Of Rolls-Royce manufacture with Bijur pinion and 9.15:1 planetary reduction with friction-drive clutch device.

Instruments

Petrol gauge, ammeter, oil pressure gauge, water temperature gauge, combined revolution counter and clock, speedometer.

Cooling system

Forced pump circulation and belt-driven four-blade fan, thermostatically (Calostat) controlled radiator shutters. Capacity 24 pints (13.638 litres).

Petrol system

Twin SU petrol-pumps working in tandem mounted on bulkhead, 18 gallon (81.9 litres) tank with 2 gallon (9.1 litres) reserve controlled from inside bulkhead switch. Later model with dashboard switch for A or B or both pumps.

TRANSMISSION

Gearbox

Four forward speeds and reverse with synchromesh on third and top. Right-hand gate change.
Ratios: Reverse 11.15:1; First, 2.76:1; Second, 1.73:1; Third, 1.24:1, Top, direct. 1935: isolated gear lever.
Oil capacity: 4½ pints (2.56 litres).

Clutch

Single dry plate with direct foot operation (Rolls-Royce manufacture) 9⅞in (251mm).

Propeller shaft

Single-piece open type with two all-metal universal joints (needle type in 1936).

Rear axle and final drive

Open fully floating with hypoid spiral bevel gears, giving engine to road wheel ratio in top, normal 10/41 (4.10:1), optional 11/43 (3.909:1). Torque reaction taken by road springs. Oil capacity 1½ pints (0.85 litres).

CHASSIS

Frame

Channel section designed to give a low centre of gravity.

Suspension

Semi-elliptical leaf springs to front and rear.

Shock absorbers

Hydraulic lever-arm type manufactured by Rolls-Royce, both front and rear. 1934 rear dampers adjusted by steering column hand control powered by gearbox pump and centrifugally controlled to increase damper loading with road speed.

Brakes

Pedal-operated, mechanical internal expanding on all four wheels via patented friction-disc type servo. Independent handbrake operating on rear wheels only with separate shoes; rear wheels have four shoes each. Front anti-judder bob weights fitted, except to very early models. Cast-aluminium shoes.

Front axle

'H'-section high-tensile steel.

Steering

Worm and nut.

Chassis lubrication

One-shot pedal-operated chassis lubricating system with 2 pint (1.136 litres) capacity tank on bulkhead.

Exhaust system

Single-piece manifold to front expansion box to two silencers and tailpipe. Exhaust cut-out available with control from centre of floor.

Wheels

Detachable centre-lock wire wheels with well-base rims; early models Dunlop, later Rudge-Whitworth. Right- and left-hand threaded hubcaps.

Tyres

India Speed Special 5.50in x 18in (140mm x 457.2mm) with India special black tubes.

PRINCIPAL CHASSIS DETAILS AND DIMENSIONS

Wheelbase: 10ft 6in (3.2m).
Track: 4ft 8in (1.42m).
Overall length: 14ft 6in (4.42m).
Overall body width: 5ft 9in (1.75m).
Turning circle: Right 42ft (12.8m); Left 40ft 8in (12.4m).
Ground clearance: 6in (152mm).
Weight: Chassis 20cwt (1,008kg).
With Park Ward saloon body 30cwt (1,512kg).
Performance: Maximum speed 92 mph (147.2km/h).
Petrol consumption 17-18mpg.
Price at introduction: Chassis only £1,100 (wheel discs £20 extra).
Four-door saloon £1,460.
Number built: 1,177.
Radiator badge: Black enamel background and winged 'B' mascot on radiator cap.

3½-Litre AXX286

Chassis No: B11AE   Engine No: Z6BA   Registered: April 1934

Manufactured in 1933, the sixth Bentley chassis produced by Rolls-Royce and registered in April 1934. It was at that time fitted with a Vanden Plas tourer body, the owner being Mrs Smith-Bingham of Banbury, England. At some later date a Sedanca de Ville body was fitted (photograph opposite) by a maker unknown. As can be seen, at the time the photograph was taken the car was in a very poor state. A little later in its life, AXX 286 was involved in a serious accident, bending front axle and chassis frame, and writing off the already rotted body. It was then allowed to freeze up, bursting the cylinder head. At this stage Mr C.B.D. Sargent of Kent purchased the remains in 1962, mainly in order to obtain

the opera lamps! A year or two later Mr Sargent decided to rebuild the chassis and build and fit a two-seater body. Designing the type of body he had in mind proved to be almost impossible with such a long wheelbase, so he reduced the length by 12in (306.5mm) and at the same time shortened the radiator and bulkhead by 4in (102mm). He then designed and built the third body to be fitted to the chassis. The car was back on the road in August 1966 and won the 3½-litre class at Kensington Gardens in June 1967 and 1972, and the class for open Derby-built cars in 1975. The photograph below bears witness to the excellent job done by Mr Sargent.

3½-Litre AXK5

AXK 5 supplied to Mr R.C. Stewart of London with a standard open tourer body by Vanden Plas for the cost of £1,397 7s 6d against which an allowance was made of £186 for the sale of an 8-litre by Mr P.M. Stewart (this must have been GY 88 – chassis YX5117, engine YX5120, now owned by Mr Briggs Cunningham of California, USA). The car is now owned by Mr K. Wilyman of Sutton Coldfield, England. Some modifications have been carried out including the removal of the standard air cleaner from the carburettors and the fitting of individual cleaners to each carburettor as shown in the photograph on the facing page. The car was featured in 'Automobile Quarterly's 'Great Cars and Grand Marques', and is used regularly by its owner. The picture below shows (left to right) H.N. Harben, Mrs W.O. Bentley, R. Whitehouse, N. Hood, W.O. Bentley, Stanley Sedgwick and K. Wilyman admiring AXK 5 at a meeting at Droitwich Spa, England, in 1970.

3½-Litre CJJ190

Chassis No: B45AE   Engine No: T9BG   Registered: April 1934

This car's first owner was HRH Prince George KG, GCVO (later Duke of Kent), and the body was specially built by Barker & Co (Coachbuilders) Ltd who were the agents for the sale. Only the chassis price – £1,100 – is shown on the works card. The use of the car was described as touring in England. One special specification was that speedometer and revolution counter should be on the left of the instrument board. Pictures of the car appeared in the English press at the time of Prince George's marriage to Princess Marina when they left in it for their honeymoon. The car is now owned by Mr J. Lyden Henton who lives in Surrey, England. The picture on the left shows Prince George (taller central figure) with the car at Olympia. When the Duke of Kent sold this car and had a 4¼-litre Bentley in its place he transferred the registration AXL 1 to his new car and chassis B45AE was re-registered as CJJ 190.

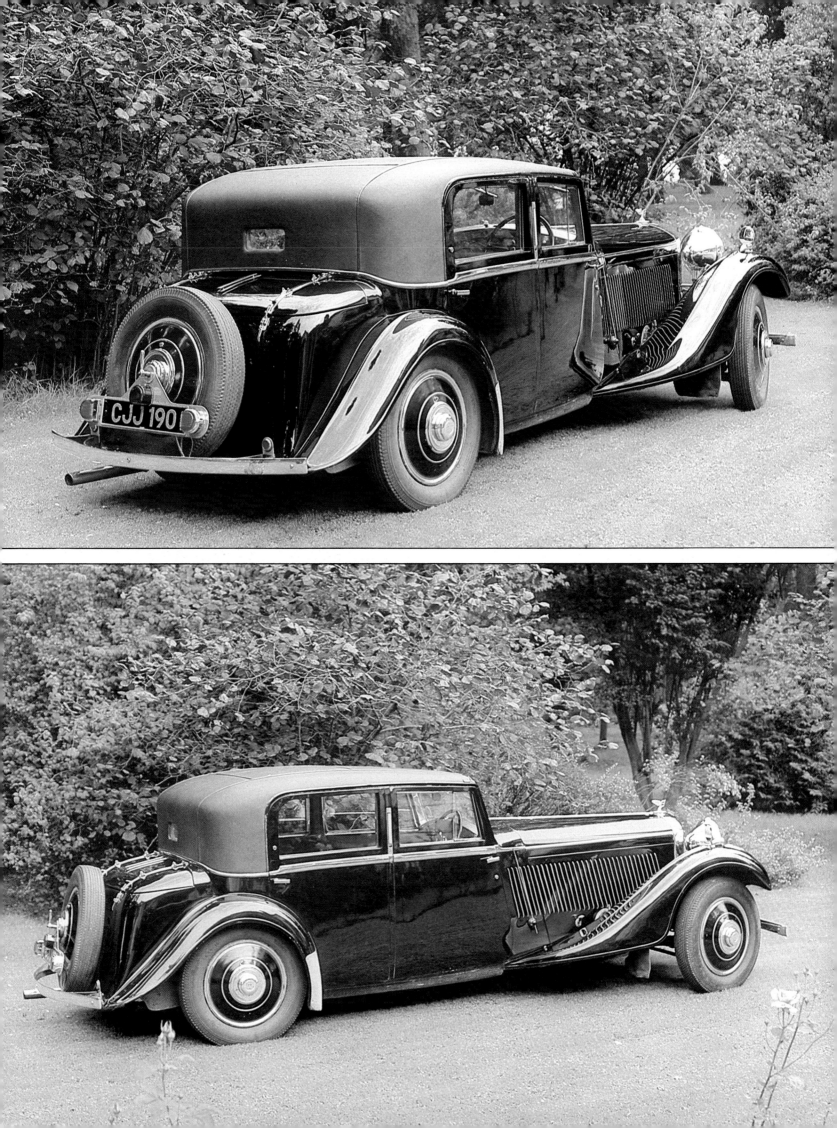

3½-Litre 691ABO

Chassis No: B69BL   Engine No: X6BD   Registered: September 1934

A very elegant three-seater drop-head coupé body by Vanden Plas built for Miss Frances A. Rolls of Eastbourne and now owned by Mrs Eileen Smith of Somerset, England. The original works card states that the car was for UK and Continental touring and one special requirement was that the change gear and brake levers should be set back 2in (50mm) further from the dash than standard position. The photograph, bottom right, shows an interesting aperture for the taxation disc.

145

3½-Litre SGO29

Chassis No: B43BN   Engine No: B9BA   Registered: December 1934

This car with a two-seater coupé cabriolet body built by Hooper & Co (Coachbuilders) Ltd was specially designed for Baron R. Gendebein of Belgium and was exhibited at the Brussels Motor Show from 24 November to 5 December 1934. It was returned to the works after the show for minor modifications and shipped back to Belgium from London on SS 'City of London' on 29 December 1934. Special requirements were a speedometer in kilometres, petrol gauge in litres and headlamps to dip vertically. The Belgian registration number was 349D4. The car returned from Belgium and was registered SGO 29 on 2 November 1955. It is now in the Fuad Majzub Collection in Worcestershire, England. On the opposite page are Hooper's official photograph and drawings of the car.

Following spread: SGO 29 in its present home.

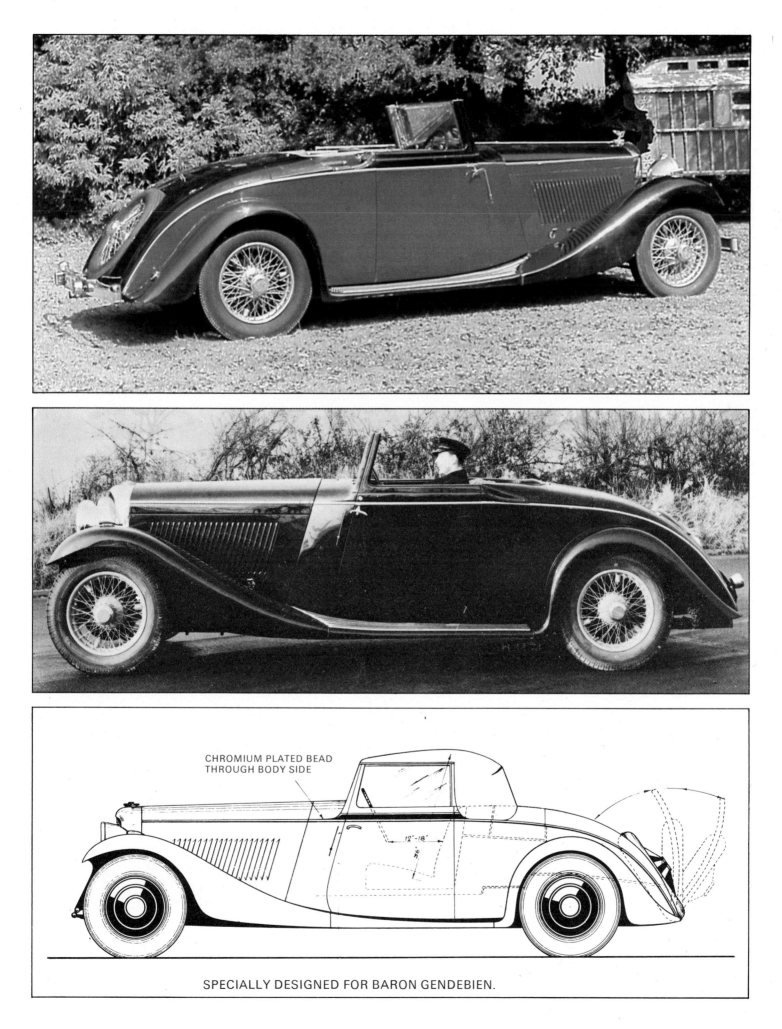

CHROMIUM PLATED BEAD
THROUGH BODY SIDE

SPECIALLY DESIGNED FOR BARON GENDEBIEN.

3½-Litre CGH743

Chassis No: B119EJ   Engine No: F6BA   Registered: October 1935

This car was first owned by a Mr R.S. Rogers of London who ordered it through Jack Barclay Ltd. The works card states that a Thrupp and Maberly foursome drop-head coupé body was to be supplied, but in the event a four-door sports saloon was fitted from new and the original body is still on it. Records indicate that this car which is now owned by John Adams of Worcestershire, England, has been taxed and on the road all its life except for twelve months during 1971-72 when springs, shock absorbers and steering were completely overhauled. The total mileage so far covered by this car exceeds 450,000 miles (724,050km). As will be seen from the picture below, the car originally had Ace discs fitted, which were removed by the present owner. The car has attended

many Bentley Drivers Club meetings over the last few years. The picture below was taken in 1967 shortly after being acquired by the present owner.

Facing page:

Top left: By the 113-year-old narrow-gauge locomotive of the Talyllyn Railway in Wales.

Top and middle right: Touring in France 1977, equipped with orange headlamp glasses for European night driving.

Bottom right: By a Welsh lake.

3½-Litre CGX344

Chassis No: B140FB　　　**Engine No: S4BN**　　　**Registered: January 1936**

This Sedanca coupé by Hooper (Coachbuilders) Ltd was supplied to a Mr J.C. Piddock who kept the car until January 1939. The present owner, Mr M.B. Gaudin of Devonshire, England, bought it in 1971. The body has some unusual features: one, being a Sedanca, the two doors have no top to the window frames, and the other the opening back window, a sure method of getting good ventilation!

3½-Litre BOP 600

This open four-seater Continental tourer by Vanden Plas was delivered in April 1936 to the first owner Mr S.K. Thornley, and it has been owned by his son M.D. Thornley since his father's death in 1947. The Thornley family have always been great Bentley enthusiasts starting with a 3-litre in 1924, followed by a 1928 4½-litre Vanden Plas four-seater, a 1930 Speed Six with a Salmon's saloon, a 1934 3½-litre Hooper saloon, then BOP 600 and finally a 1938 4¼-litre, but only BOP 600 remains. BOP 600 was a competitor in the 1936-37-38-39 and 1951 RAC Scottish Rallies and was in a pre-war Le Touquet Concours. The car has always been used for everyday motoring and during the war on one occasion it was pressed into service for a night-time dash into Birmingham to remove company records from the family factory, which was in danger during a heavy blitz. Between 1948 and 1962 the car was used for many Continental tours of 2,000 miles (3,220km) or more and has visited most European countries, not to mention a tour of Iceland, when very rough roads were encountered. The car is still used four days a week to commute eighteen miles into Birmingham and back and Mr Thornley boasts that the hood has not been up for three years! It is not surprising therefore to learn that this car has covered nearly 550,000 miles (885,500km) from new.

The pictures below show BOP 600 during the 1938 Scottish Rally taking the test near Strathpeffer and at the Glasgow Exhibition. The bottom picture shows the dashboard covered with rally competitor's badges. The present owner Mr David Thornley lives in Warwickshire, England.

4¼-Litre

In 1935, W.O. Bentley left Rolls-Royce to join Lagonda. So when in 1936 the larger 4¼-litre model was announced, the tie between Bentley the man and Bentley the machine was severed. He remained with Lagonda, later amalgamated with Aston-Martin, until after the end of the Second World War.

The larger engine, which was initially intended as an option, at £50 extra, was immediately adopted as standard. *Motor* road-tested a 4¼-engined car, fitted with a Park Ward saloon body and on 21 April 1936 reported that 'a flying quarter-mile was covered at Brooklands at a time speed of 96mph (154.46km/h) and 0 to 50mph (0 to 80.45km/h), through the gears, in 10.6 secs.' It was, said the report, 'Altogether an extremely satisfactory car, which provides a unique combination of verve with docility, speed with comfort, and performance with silence.'

The 4,257cc-engined car was able to give a good account of itself on the British roads, but on the Continent the development of the new autobahn and autostrada in Germany and Italy gave the sporting owner on the 'Grand Tour' the chance to keep his foot hard down for long periods on those straight, open roads. Consequently, crankshaft bearings and oil systems were improved to cope with the extra demand on performance. The improvements enabled the engine to run for long periods at up to 4,500rpm without any problem. The servo-assisted brakes introduced on the 3½ proved smooth and effective with low pedal pressures, and were well able to match the extra power. However, it was felt that a change in gearing would be an improvement and in 1938 the overdrive gearbox was fitted, starting with the MR series. At the same time a lower back-axle ratio was fitted, which meant that the opposition, in the form of the 3½-litre Delahaye, 500 Mercedes, Type 57 Bugatti, the Paris-

Nice Hotchkiss, and perhaps the 4-litre Talbot, could be matched.

During 1938, Walter Sleator, Manager of the Paris branch of Rolls-Royce, Franco Brittanic Autos, commissioned a $4\frac{1}{4}$, with a carefully prepared but standard chassis and a streamlined body, for Mr A.M.Embiricos, a Greek racing driver. It was intended for high-speed touring and use on the autobahn. The body was designed by M. Georges Paulin, together with Van Vooren who built the body, and it proved to be a very fast and handsome car. It was capable of averaging 112mph (180.20km/h) and, in fact, with Captain G.E.T. Eyston driving, it covered 114.63 miles (184.45km) in one hour at Brooklands. It was later purchased in July 1939, by H.S.F. Hay, and after the war it was entered in a number of races. In 1949, the car, driven by J. Hay and T.H. Wisdom, made an appearance at Le Mans, where it finished sixth, at 73.56mph (118.39km/h). Again in 1950, Hay competed at Le Mans in this streamlined car, with H. Hunter as his co-driver. They finished twelfth at 78.60mph (126.47km/h). By this time modern machinery was becoming more sophisticated, and because there was little chance of the car finishing high in the field, it did not appear again.

A total of 1,234 cars were built on the $4\frac{1}{4}$-litre chassis and these included 202 with overdrive gearbox on the MR and MX series of 1938 and 1939. These particular cars had 6.50 tyres on 17 inch (165 x 431mm) wheels, and a lower geared Marles steering box.

Taking everything into consideration the post-vintage Bentleys were fine cars, entirely satisfying that section of the motoring public in a time of leisure and elegance for which they were designed, the like of which we shall probably never see again.

Above: A very nice Freestone and Webb Razor Edge saloon, chassis No B144JD, engine No R4BS, originally registered DXE 44. This car is now owned by Mr N.W. Stickney of Minnesota, USA.

Below: The ultimate in $4\frac{1}{4}$-litre standard chassis cars. This body built by Pourtout of Paris for Mr A.M. Embericos was on chassis No B27LE with engine No L9BC which was delivered to the coachbuilders in July 1938. With registration No 2RL9, it is here seen at speed at Brooklands in July 1929, with Captain G.E.T. Eyston at the wheel when it covered ten miles (16.09km) at 115.05mph (185.15km/h).

Facing page: A $4\frac{1}{4}$-litre test rig at the Derby Works of Rolls-Royce Ltd in 1935.

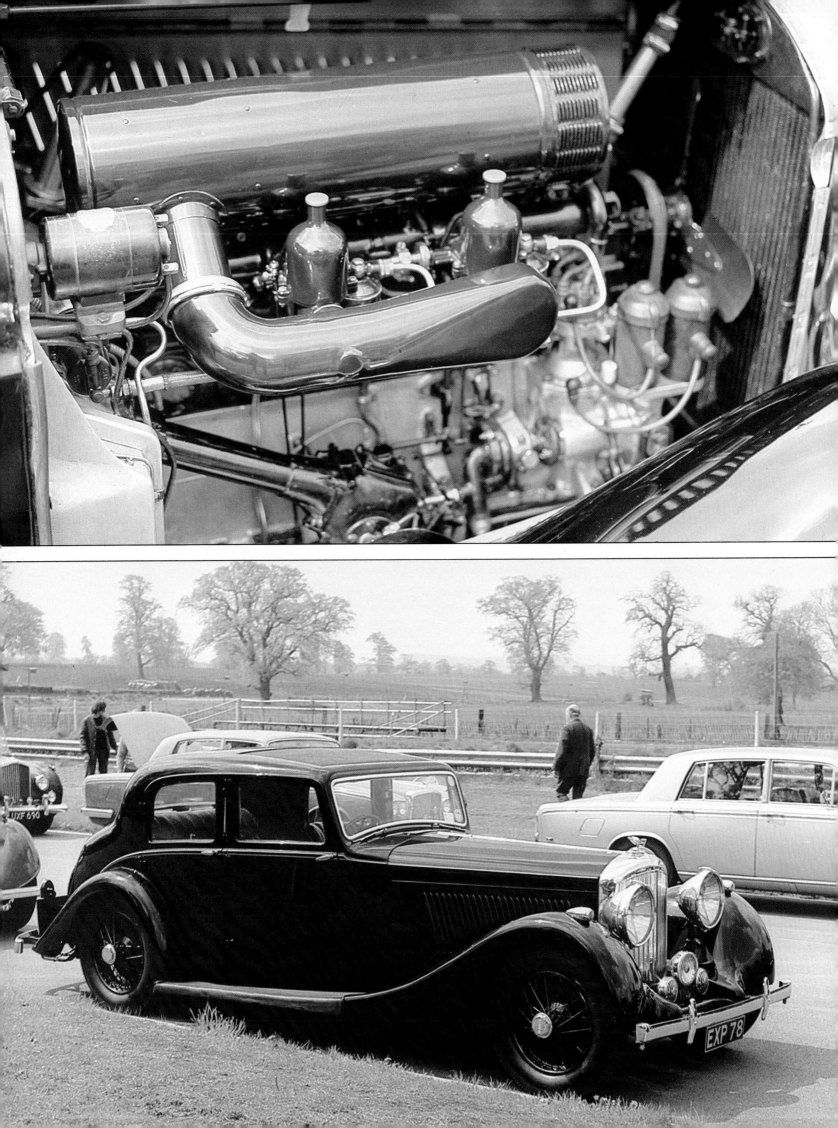

SPECIFICATION

4¼-LITRE

In production 1936-40.

Basic specification at introduction (with some production modifications) – many details are the same as for the 3½-litre and are therefore not shown.

ENGINE
6 cylinders; firing order 1, 4, 2, 6, 3, 5 (as 3½-litre).

Bore	3¼in (89mm)
Stroke	4½in (114mm)
Cubic capacity	4,257cc (260cu in)
Compression ratio	6.8:1
Brake horsepower	125 (approximate)
RAC rating	29.4hp

Crankshaft
As 3½-litre, except that Hall Metal used for bearings.

Lubrication
As 3½-litre, except most M series cars had by-pass oil filter, and large-capacity pump fitted to later cars.

Carburettors
Twin 1⅝in (41mm) SUs HV4 type.

Dynamo
Positive drive at 1½-times engine speed from camshaft gear two-brush air-cooled with automatic regulator type B2 CJ 1A/11 dynamo of Rolls-Royce manufacture to 1 x 12 volt 55 amp hour battery.

Instruments
As 3½-litre, except addition of green fuel warning light to indicate only 2 gallons (9.1 litres) left, no reserve control switch.

Cooling system
As 3½-litre, except MR and MX series cars had fixed radiator shutters.

Petrol system
As 3½-litre.

TRANSMISSION
Gearbox
As for 3½-litre, except MR and MX series cars which have different ratios and an overdrive top.

Ratios: Reverse, 10.63:1; First, 2.38:1; Second, 1.49:1; Third, 1:1; Top, 08.5:1.
Oil capacity: 4 pints (2.28 litres).

Clutch
Borg and Beck 10in (254mm) single dry plate.

Propeller shaft
As 3½-litre.

Rear axle and final drive
As 3½-litre, except MR and MX series had engine to road wheel ratio in top of 10 43 (43:1). Oil capacity 1½ pints (0.85 litres).

CHASSIS
Brakes
As 3½-litre, except for modified balance weight to front linkage.

Steering
As 3½ litre, except MR and MX series which have Marles cam and roller.

Wheels
As 3½-litre, except MR and MX series – see tyre sizes.

Tyres
To 1938 5.50in x 18in (140mm x 457mm) India Super.
MR/MX series 6.50in x 17in (165mm x 432mm) India Silent.

PRINCIPAL CHASSIS DETAILS AND DIMENSIONS
Weight: 21cwt (1,058kg).
With Park Ward steel saloon body 33½cwt (1,688kg).
Performance: Standard car: Maximum speed 96mph (153.6km/h).
Petrol consumption 17-19mpg.
MR/MX series: Maximum speed 107mph (171.2km/h).
Petrol consumption 16-18mpg.

Below: A 4¼-litre chassis.

Facing page:

Above: A 4¼-litre engine in chassis B133LE.

Below: A Park Ward saloon on a 4¼-litre chassis: more Park Ward bodies were supplied for this model than any other make. This car EXP 78 is now owned by Mr J.D. Sharp of Gloucestershire, England.

4¼-Litre CXK1

Chassis No: B22GA   Engine No: U2BM   Registered: April 1936

CXK 1 is one of the more notable 4¼-litre Bentleys. Supplied new to Sir Malcolm Campbell, the holder of both land and water world speed records in his famous 'Bluebirds', this was one of Sir Malcolm's favourite cars. He wrote of this car 'The engine, steering, suspension and brakes are absolute perfection. I have never driven a car that holds the road so well – the 4¼-litre Bentley is the most amazing proposition which it has ever fallen my lot to handle.' The original works card says 'Special attention to chassis, a very fast car wanted'. CXK 1 went to the USA in 1959 and since 1960 has been owned by Mr G.L. Steward Jr of Massachusetts who has restored the car to new condition. The body is one of the classic Vanden Plas four-seater sports tourers which suit the 4¼-litre chassis so well. The picture top right shows the car while still owned by Sir Malcolm Campbell. All the other pictures were taken in America. The car is now painted British racing green.

4¼-Litre AXL1

Chassis No: B142HK   Engine No: E7BE   Registered: February 1937

This was the Duke of Kent's second Derby-built Bentley. On this occasion he chose a special body to be built by Hoopers (Coachbuilders) Ltd, which was a four-door saloon with a division. A division in this type of body makes the rear passenger area seem very cramped. The requirements for the car were that it should be suitable for fast Continental touring. Another special requirement was for large and powerful headlamps. There is no revolution counter among the instruments and the dashboard is polished aluminium. AXL 1 is now owned by Mr P.W.R. Bull who lives in Suffolk, England.

Following spread: Another view of AXL 1.

4¼-Litre DXK2

Chassis No: B74JD   **Engine No: A4BJ**   **Registered: April 1937**

This car has an unusual body by James Young & Co Ltd of Bromley Kent built for the Hon R.R.W.S. Stoner of Henley-on Thames. It is a four-seater drop-head with parallel opening doors; a type that was described in the 'Motor' dated 7 June 1938 as 'doors without hinges, being supported at the centre on pivot arms, which swing the door outwards and sideways, giving easy access to the rear seats'. The car is kept in first-class condition by its present owner Mr R. Newill of Shropshire, England.

4¼-Litre B3044

Chassis No: B156KT   **Engine No: E9BH**   **Registered: September 1937**

Once in a while someone comes up with a truly exotic and beautiful body on a motor car. This could happen more frequently on a Bentley chassis if it were not for the more conservative outlook of those who buy cars in this class. Claude Lang of Brussels is an exception: he obviously allowed coachbuilders Vesters et Neirinck of Brussels to have their head – and what a beautiful result has been achieved with this two-seater coupé with sliding roof on 4¼-litre chassis delivered in September 1937. Claude Lang has owned this car from new and fortunately it survived the war undamaged. M Lang left his car in his garage in May 1940 and his house in Brussels was occupied by the Germans while he was in the Belgian Army in the UK. Before leaving he had removed and hidden the wheels. In addition the car was fitted with a secret main switch which meant the Germans were unable to use it; all they did was to remove the battery and the two horns. At the end of the war M Lang treated his car to a complete overhaul by the Rolls-Royce agents in Brussels.

168

4¼-Litre DYM800

Chassis No: B129JY   **Engine No: T7BR**   **Registered: August 1937**

A very lovely three-position drop-head coupé body built by J. Gurney Nutting & Co Ltd of Chelsea, London, for the first owner Miss Josefina Tarafa from Cuba. It is not known if this car ever went to Cuba, but it is unlikely as the works card says the car was required for 'UK touring', but it was shipped to France on SS 'Canterbury' on 2 November 1937. The car is now owned by Captain J. Gordon of London and was displayed at the Bentley Drivers Club Annual Ball at the Dorchester Hotel, London, in 1974.

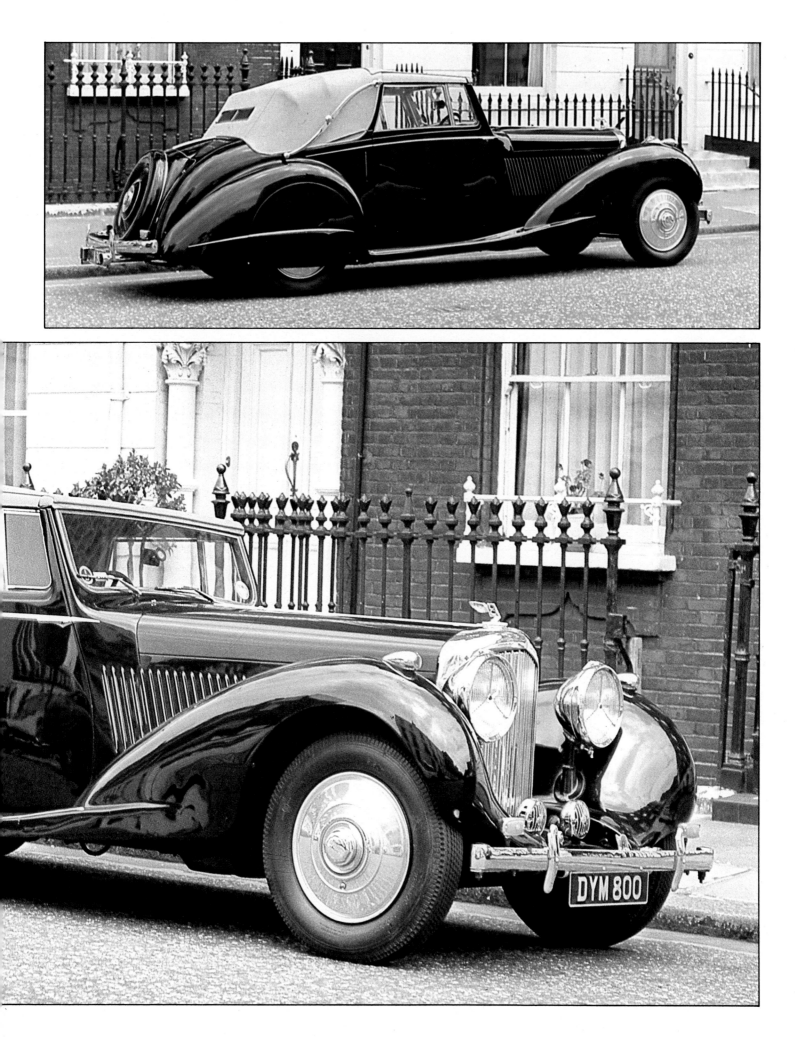

4¼-Litre ELR499

This car, bodied by Park Ward Ltd of Willesden with a pillarless razor-edge saloon, was supplied to Jack Barclay Ltd for their showroom in September 1937. It was sold to the first owner Dr Howard Butler of Bristol in January 1938. One unusual feature is a polished aluminium dashboard. The photographs of the car were taken on a tour of France in 1977 when the car was owned by Mr D.L. Hamblin of Staffordshire, England.

172

4¼-Litre FLH777

Chassis No: B95LE   Engine No: D3BK   Registered: January 1939

A sleek standard coupé built by H.J. Mulliner & Co Ltd of Chiswick, London, was supplied by Jack Barclay Ltd to a Mr N.A. Bronstein of London. He must have been very proud of his car, because he entered the concours at the RAC Rally at Brighton on 6 May 1939, where it would seem from the photograph (opposite top) he was an award winner. The car is still in very good hands, it is owned by Mr J.S. Elvins of Worcestershire, England.

4¼-Litre FLR386

Chassis No: B25MX   Engine No: S9BV   Registered: March 1939

A standard Vanden Plas open four-seater tourer on the overdrive chassis was in 1939 a very desirable motor car – as it is today. According to the works record card this body had been fitted to chassis B152LS and remounted on B25MX, a saloon body was fitted to B152LS. The original owner was a Mr H.D. Clark. The car is now owned by Mr B.M. Russ-Turner of Surrey, England, who has fitted 17in (433mm) wheels, in place of the usual 18in (457mm), which run on 670 x 16 RS5 tyres.

3½/4¼-Litre AXN373

Chassis No: B35AE   Engine No:X5BC   Registered: February 1934

Early in 1934 E.R. (Eddie) Hall the well-known racing driver purchased this 3½-litre Bentley, which was fitted with a sporting four-seater body built by E.D. Abbott Ltd of Farnham, and took it over to Italy to use as a practice car in the Mille Miglia – he was driving an MG in the race. When he returned he wrote to Rolls-Royce to tell them that the Bentley had covered over 4,000 miles (6,436km) at racing speeds over the mountain passes of the course. The outcome of this was that Eddie Hall asked Rolls-Royce if he might race the car in the 1934 Ulster TT. Although they had not raced since 1906 Rolls-Royce agreed, and certain modifications were carried out. Hall finished second at an average speed of 78mph (125.5km/h) the fastest time for the course, but was placed second on handicap, being 9mph (14.48km/h) faster than a 4½-litre supercharged Cricklewood car. This was only the beginning of an interesting career. In 1936 one of the new 4¼-litre engines was fitted to B35AE and a new two-seater body. Between 1934 and 1939 chassis B35AE was never beaten in its class in any event in which it entered. Hall raced the car again in 1950 at Le Mans with a suitably streamlined hard-top fitted, and finished eighth after a solo drive in his sixteen-year-old car. B35AE is now in the Briggs Cunningham Collection in California, USA. The colour pictures were all taken in 1977: the black and white picture shows Eddie Hall driving his car in the 1935 Ulster TT.

Mark V & Corniche

One of the few things that the late model $4\frac{1}{4}$ overdrive car lacked was independent suspension, needed to maintain high average speeds over Continental roads. Success with the modified 1938 'Embiricos' car which was fitted with a streamlined body, encouraged the factory to develop the Mark V in 1939. Among many changes were coilspring and wishbone independent front suspension on a very much stiffer and stronger chassis, together with an improved engine placed further forward in the frame. The pistons fitted to this engine had specially raised crowns, enabling a higher compression ratio to be used. Another innovation was a flywheel attached to the crankshaft by a thin flexible steel disc, which considerably reduced vibration. The gearbox had a synchromesh device making easy changes possible between overdrive, direct and second speeds; because of the increased drive-shaft length, a divided propshaft was used, supported by a flexibly mounted centre bearing. The car had a wheelbase of 10ft 4in (3.15m) and used 6.50 tyres (165mm) on 16in (406.4mm) wheels.

Many new technical developments resulted in a motor car well able to carry the company into the next decade. The prototype car, intended as a standard production type, performed excellently under all conditions, and a bright future for it seemed assured. An appearance at the 1939 Motor Show was planned but this was prevented by the outbreak of war. At the same time, a further design was evolved by the works' experimental department. The success of the special Hay car, based on the $4\frac{1}{4}$ chassis encouraged H.I.F. Evernden to develop another Mk V prototype for very fast touring;

Max Millar's drawing of a Mark V chassis for 'Autocar'.

it was to be called the Corniche and the famous test car was registered GRA 270.

The Corniche is an area on the South Coast of France, between Nice and Genoa, which takes its name from the early carriage roads, especially the Menton section built on Napoleon's orders, and it was a popular holiday venue for British people in the period between the two World Wars. It seemed most appropriate that a car eminently suitable for the journey should take the name Corniche since it was following in the steps of one of the finest motor cars built with 'Grand Touring' in mind, the 1931 Phantom II Rolls-Royce Continental.

The body of the new Bentley was designed and built by M Georges Paulin and Carrossier Van Vooren, and the intention was that it should be made by Park Ward as a production model, built on a light chassis. This particular car had a special engine with overhead inlet and side exhaust valves, and many other details of its specification broke new ground, such as the steel disc wheels, with five-bolt attachment. Sadly however, it did not return from development testing on the Continent: it was destroyed by enemy

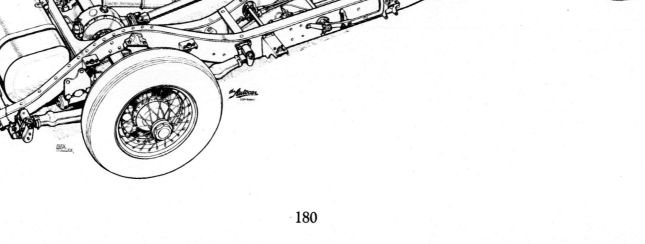

action in 1939 on the quay at Dieppe while awaiting shipment home.

Development of the two cars, the standard Mark V and the Corniche, was halted by the war. Fewer than 20 complete chassis were produced, the last one being registered in July 1940. Records exist to show that experiments were in hand with a single overhead-camshaft ramphead engine which had sodium-cooled exhaust valves. A further point of interest on the competition side was that a team of eight-cylinder engined, short chassis cars was planned for the 1940 Le Mans race and testing work was carried out in the Sarthe, but war prevented any further progress and the idea was not revived in the post-war years. However there is no doubt that the Mk V provided much of the basic design information utilised by the factory when they launched the Mark VI saloon after the war.

Above: Mark V chassis No B34AW, engine No K8BF, registration No FYL 811, owned by Mr A. Wood of Essex, England. It is fitted with a Park Ward four-door steel saloon body and was intended for the New York World's Fair but was acquired by Jack Barclay Ltd of London in June 1940 and registered JB1. Barclay's sold it to a Mr P. G. Hingley of Worcestershire, England, in October 1942 and after six further owners it was acquired by Mr Andrew Wood of Essex, England, in 1964.

SPECIFICATION

MARK V

In production 1939-40.

Basic specification at introduction:

ENGINE
6 cylinders; firing order 1, 4, 2, 6, 3, 5.

Bore:	3½in (89mm).
Stroke:	4½in (114mm).
Cubic capacity:	4,257cc (260cu in).
Compression ratio:	6.4:1.
Brake horsepower:	125 (approximate).
RAC rating:	29.4hp.

Valves and camshaft
Two valves per cylinder, overhead, operated by push-rods and rockers from camshaft, situated in the crankcase, driven by helical gears.

Cylinder block and pistons
Monobloc of cast-iron with detachable cast-iron cylinder head. Alloy pistons with raised crown.

Crankcase and sump
Aluminium crankcase and one-piece aluminium sump.

Crankshaft
Mounted in seven white metal bearings. Big-end bearings made in RR-AC9 white metal. Safe maximum rpm 4,500.

Lubrication
Pressure feed to crankshaft bearings, gudgeon pins and valve rockers. By-pass filter. Sump capacity 14 pints (7.96 litres).

Ignition
Coil via ballast resistance. Automatic advance and retard controlled by centrifugal governor in distributor (fitted to near side of engine) to one sparking plug per cylinder on off side of engine. Some cars had over-riding hand advance and retard. 14mm sparking plugs.

Carburettors
Twin SU carburettors fitted with thermostatic water-heated inlet manifold on off side of engine, operating automatically on cold start.

Dynamo
Positive drive from timing gears. Automatic regulator, vibrator control. Rolls-Royce manufacture. 12 volt to 55 amp hour battery.

Starter
Rolls-Royce manufacture with pinion providing gentle engagement via reduction gear.

Instruments
Speedometer, revolution counter, clock, radiator thermometer, fuel gauge, oil pressure gauge, ammeter.

Cooling system
Forced pump circulation with thermostatic control and belt-driven fan. Water-pump fitted to near side of engine shaft driven from dynamo. Capacity 24 pints (13.65 litres).

Petrol system
Dual electric pump mounted on off side of chassis frame. 16 gallon (72.8 litres) tank.

TRANSMISSION
Gearbox
Four forward speeds and reverse, synchromesh on second, third

and top. Right-hand gate change.

> Ratios: Reverse, 2.47:1; First, 2.44:1; Second, 1.43:1; Third, 1:1; Top (overdrive), 0.836:1.
> Oil capacity: 5 pints (2.84 litres).

Clutch
Single dry plate to flexibly mounted flywheel.

Propeller shaft
Open two-piece with sealed intermediate flexibly mounted bearing. Needle type universal joints.

Rear axle and final drive
Fully floating hypoid gear with bevel differential giving engine to road wheel ratio in top of 10/43 (4.3:1).

> Torque reaction taken by road springs.

CHASSIS
Frame
Deep channel-section side frame with box-section 'X' bracing. Bulkhead mounted by bi-plane support bushes.

Suspension
Semi-elliptical leaf springs to rear and independent front with wishbones and coil springs.

Shock absorbers
Hydraulic piston type of Rolls-Royce manufacture to all four wheels. Rear centrifugally controlled with over-riding hand control of steering column. Front dampers forming top wishbone arms.

Brakes
Four-wheel mechanical (Girling wedge and roller expander) with mechanical gearbox-driven friction servo. Handbrake to rear wheels. 14in (355.5mm) diameter brake-drums.

Front axle
Independent front suspension with helical springs and triangulated wishbones, lower rear member acting as brake torque member.

Steering
Cam and roller.

Chassis lubrication
One-shot pedal-operated chassis lubrication system with 2 pint (1.14 litres) capacity tank on bulkhead.

Exhaust system
Single three-branch manifold with single pipe to expansion box, silencer and tailpipe.

Wheels
Detachable centre-lock wire wheels (well-base) with left- and right-hand thread locking caps.

Tyres
Avon 6.50in x 16in (165mm x 406.5mm).

PRINCIPAL CHASSIS DETAILS AND DIMENSIONS
Wheelbase: 10ft 4in (3.15m).
Track: Front 4ft 8¼in (1.44m); Rear 4ft 10in (1.47m).
Overall length: 15ft 11in (4.85m).
Overall body width: 5ft 9in (1.75m).
Turning circle: Right 43ft (13.11m); Left 44ft 4in (13.51m).
Ground clearance: 6½in (165mm).
Weight: Chassis 24.26cwt (1,210-1,310kg) with Park Ward steel saloon.
Performance: Maximum speed 97mph (155.2km/h).
Petrol consumption: 17-19mpg.
Price at introduction: Chassis only £1,150.
Four-door saloon (Parkward) £2,307.
Number built: 14 (plus four Corniche and one experimental chassis No 14BV (GRA270).
Radiator badge: Black enamel background and winged 'B' mascot on radiator cap.

Below left: Mark V development drawings.

Below: The prototype Mark V engine. From the nearside showing distributor, and dynamo driven from timing gears with water-pump and driving shaft from dynamo.

Mark V GRA 270

The main differences between the Mark V and the Corniche were that the compression ratio increased to 7.25:1; there were two valves per cylinder, overhead inlet and side exhaust valves; the cylinder block and crankcase were cast in one piece with overhead valves operated by push-rods and totally enclosed rockers; there were larger-bore twin SU carburettors; the dynamo, water pump and fan were belt driven; the fuel tank increased in size to take 19 gallons (86.45 litres); the semi-floating type rear axle had a ratio 3.73:1; twin exhaust system with two silencers and two resonators led to twin tailpipes; there were pressed-steel type wheels with five bolt fixing; the overall length was increased by 2in (50.8mm) to 15ft 11in (4.85m). Designed for a maximum speed of 109 to 120mph (175-193Kmp), one experimental and four other cars were built but none was sold. GRA 270 was despatched to France in August 1939 for testing, but never returned, having been destroyed by enemy action while on the quay at Dieppe. The coachwork and styling were by Van Vooren of Paris.

Right: One of the experimental Corniche cars came to grief on the roads of France while under test.

Below: The Bentley that might have been: the Corniche before leaving for test in France.

Mark V GJ88

Chassis No: B30 AW   **Engine No: B9 HP**   **Registered: October 1947**

A standard Mark V chassis it was on test at the Derby factory on 18 August 1939 and was sent to H.J. Mulliner Ltd on 31 August 1939 for the body. This car was originally ordered by Car Mart Ltd of London and intended for their stand at the 1939 Motor Show at Olympia, London, which was cancelled because of the outbreak of war. It was stored by Mulliner's until 1945 when the body work was completed for Rolls-Royce with an H.J. Mulliner touring saloon body. It was first registered with No HGH 178 in the name of Dr F. Llewellyn Smith of Rolls-Royce. It had five further owners before being acquired in May 1966 by Mr M.J. Ellman-Brown of Kent, England, who still owns it. During the course of its life the registration number was changed to GJ 88.

Mark VI

The following advertisement appeared in the April 1942 edition of *Autocar*. 'The facilities devoted in times of peace to the manufacture of Bentley Cars are now concentrated on vital war production. At some time in the future the Bentley will again become a peace-time product. It will then be found that the experience acquired during further years of research and development in other engineering fields has been blended into a car which will excel even the rightly famed pre-war product.'

Through the war years the parent company had been hard at work providing the aircraft engines to power Battle of Britain fighters, and subsequently supplying engines to the British bomber force. The skills and costs of labour employed in industry had matured and increased considerably, accelerated by the demands of survival. The cost of producing a coachbuilt car in any volume, bearing in mind the austerity which existed after the war, seemed likely to be astronomical and the large-engined cars still suffered from the penalty of the horsepower tax, based on the RAC rating formula, first levied in 1919, not to mention the very high levels of personal taxation, and stringent petrol rationing.

The strong future that the Mark VI was to have was possibly helped in some small way by the fact that the government abolished the horsepower tax in January 1948 and levied a flat rate of £10 per car. Despite all the problems besetting the motor industry, the factory was determined to restart car manufacture. The first post-war Bentley, a Mk VI, appeared in May 1946 and it was offered as a complete four-door, four-light saloon, an entirely new departure, and no doubt the drawing office at Park Ward, which had become part of Rolls-Royce in 1939, had no small part in its design. The chassis carried a three-year warranty, similar to that given to the pre-war Derby-built cars.

The end of the war had seen the production of the Motor Car Division being transferred from Derby to Crewe, hence the definition 'Crewe Cars'. The engine used was a six-cylinder of

Top right: A Mark VI standard steel saloon, an all steel body of Bentley Motors own design KOX 952, chassis No: 219HB, engine No: B234H, seen when in the ownership of Mr R. Norton of Birmingham, England.

Middle right: A Mark VI chassis with Sedanca coupé coachwork by Gurney Nutting Ltd described in the 1952 Bentley catalogue as being equally suitable as a smart town carriage or for long distance touring. The roof above the two front seats of this car can be moved rearwards to give the same advantages as an open car.

Right: A four-door sports saloon coachwork by H. J. Mulliner & Co Ltd.

4,256cc but while it had the same bore and stroke as the pre-war Derby engine, it was an entirely fresh design, a B60 series developed during the war, when it had been used in four- six- and eight-cylinder form in some staff lorries and cars. It had an F-Type alloy cylinder head as tried in the 1939 Corniche, and featured a belt drive for the dynamo and water-pump, this reducing the gear trains from five to two. The top half of each cylinder bore was chromium-plated, later to be replaced with a short liner with a thirty per cent chrome content. The huge X-braced chassis frame now carried hydraulic front brakes and independent front suspension; the gearbox had synchromesh on all except first gear and reverse with a direct drive top gear. Only one chassis form was offered, a 10ft (3.05m) wheelbase. This new all-steel bodied car, commonly known as a 'Standard Steel', was assembled entirely at

Above: DRX 550 – the much-travelled Mark VI of Mr Michael Collier, of Berkshire, England.

the Crewe factory, and although the Pressed Steel Company was responsible for producing the complete body shells, they were made to the drawings of the Crewe design team.

Autocar of 24 October 1947 published results of a road-test on one of the early standard steel saloons, reporting that the character of the car had been modified to a certain extent in comparison with the pre-war edition mainly by virtue of its ride characteristics having softer suspension. Nevertheless, that car was extolled for its 'magnificent qualities on the road, representing a pinnacle of motoring experience'. Praise indeed, even for a Bentley. Acceleration tests showed 0 to 50mph (0–80km/h) through the gears in 12.5 seconds, with 100mph (160km/h) showing on the speedometer at times, indicating a corrected 90mph-plus (144km/h) top speed.

In July 1947, Raymond Mays took a Mark VI on an 1,200 mile (1,930km) trip to two Grand Prix circuits at Berne and Nimes, finishing up at Montlhéry for further road-testing. During the course of this journey such men as Chiron, Varzi, Trossi and Sommer drove the car and made 'unanimous avowals of amazement at such blending of refinement and high spirits'. The factory engineers and designers had undoubtedly profited from the technologies developed during the war, when Merlin and Griffin aircraft engines had been built at the Crewe shadow factory.

Motorists and manufacturers were both relieved when on 26 May 1950 petrol rationing ended in Great Britain. The basic car had continued in production virtually unchanged for five years. In May 1951, the engine capacity was increased to 4,566cc (4½-litres) with full-flow oil filter lubrication, twin exhaust system and

other detail modifications. Shortly afterwards side-scuttle ventilators were fitted. The so-called 'Big Bore' car had entered the scene, but still with a small boot. Normal equipment of the standard saloon included heater and de-misters, leather upholstery (much of it supplied by Connolly's), radio, picnic tables, vanity mirrors and reading lights, spare coil, reverse lights, oil level indicator, fog lamp, to mention but a few items. Wheelspats and sunroof were optional extras. The distinctive radiator shell retained its basic form, proudly heading the car, although the arrangement of vertical grill slats was slightly altered on the later series cars; the coach-work was finished in a choice of six single colour schemes, and later two-tones were introduced.

All the post-war Bentleys had a 'B' surrounded by black enamel on the radiator shell, and a forward-sloping winged 'B', similar to that on the pre-war 3½ and 4¼ was fixed to a dummy radiator cap. In addition to the standard body, nearly 1,000 chassis were fitted with hand-built bodies, most of the famous coachbuilders in England adding their creations to such well known Continental names as Figoni, Facel Metalon, Ramseier and Farina. During this period Harold Radford Ltd developed its famous 'Countryman' conversions and a luxury timber-framed estate car was also exhibited in October 1948, by the same company.

In 1951 experiments were in hand to construct a Continental, based on a Mark VI, fitted originally with an overdrive gearbox and later with direct drive and higher rear axle. However, it was never completed as such, and we had to wait until the R-Type before development was perfected. In all, over 5,200 Mark VI chassis were built, and the last one was delivered to the customer on 17 September 1952.

SPECIFICATION

MARK VI (4¼-litres; 4½-litres)

In production: 4¼-litres; 1946–51
4½-litres; 1951–52

Basic specification at introduction (with some production modifications):

ENGINE
6 cylinders; firing order 1, 4, 2, 6, 3, 5.

	4¼-litres	4½-litres
Bore	3½in (89mm)	3⅝in (92mm)
Stroke	4½in (114mm)	4½in (114mm)
Cubic capacity	4,257cc (259.9cu in)	4,566cc (278.6cu in)
Compression ratio	6.4:1	6.4:1
Brake horsepower	135 (approximate)	150 (approximate)
RAC rating	29.4hp	31.5hp

Valves and camshaft
Two valves per cylinder, overhead inlet valves operated by push-rods, side exhaust valves operated by camshaft running in four babbit steel-lined shell bearings.

Cylinder block and pistons
Monobloc of cast-iron with the top of bores chromium plated. Later models had brichrome inserts in the top of cylinder. Detachable aluminium alloy cylinder head with nickel-chrome inlet-valve seats. Early models had solid skirt pistons; later models had split skirt pistons.

Crankcase and sump
Crankcase integral with cylinder block, with one-piece cast-aluminium sump.

Crankshaft

Seven bearing with copper-lead-indium-lined steel shells. Integral balance weights and combined spring-drive and friction type damper.

Lubrication

Pressure feed to all crankshaft and connecting-rod bearings with low pressure to rocker shaft. By-pass oil filter (full flow from 1951). Sump capacity 16 pints (9.1 litres).

Ignition

Coil (Lucas B12 and Delco Remy) and distributor with automatic advance and retard controlled by centrifugal governor in distributor. One sparking plug per cylinder (Champion N8 or Lodge CLN30, 14mm.)

Carburettors

Twin SUs type H4 ($1\frac{1}{4}$in; 31.75mm choke). Later $4\frac{1}{2}$-litre engine twin SU type H6 ($1\frac{3}{4}$in; 44.45mm choke). Manual choke; later cars with H6 carburettors had fully automatic cold start control.

Dynamo

Special equipment Lucas model RA5 12-volt with automatic voltage control and cut-out to 55 amp hour battery (Exide or Dagenite). Early chassis had Lucas C45PV-type dynamo.

Starter

Special equipment Lucas model M45G with planetary reduction gear and pinion to provide gentle engagement with friction clutch incorporated.

Below: 'Autocar' chassis drawing by John Ferguson.

Instruments

Fuel/oil level gauge, clock, ammeter, oil pressure gauge, water temperature, speedometer.

Cooling system

Belt-driven five-blade fan and centrifugal water-pump, thermostatic control. Fixed radiator shutters. Capacity 30 pints (17 litres).

Petrol system

Twin SU electric pumps, type L, mounted on off-side of chassis frame. Rear tank capacity 18 gallons (82 litres) with dashboard warning light when 2 gallons (9 litres) left.

TRANSMISSION
Gearbox

Four forward speeds and reverse, synchromesh on second, third and top. Right-hand gate change.
  Ratios: Reverse, 3.15:1; First, 2.98:1; Second, 2.02:1; Third, 1.34:1; Top, direct.
  Oil capacity: 6 pints (3.4 litres).

Clutch

10in (254mm) single dry plate (long type); later (1950) 11in (280mm). Borg and Beck type with Mintex H4 linings.

Propeller shaft

Divided two-piece, fitted with grease-retaining needle-bearing universal joints.

Rear axle and final drive
Semi-floating type, hypoid bevel, four-pinion differential, giving engine to rear wheel ratios in top of 11/14 (3.727:1), optional 12/31 (3.41:1).
Oil capacity 1¾ pints (0.9 litres).

CHASSIS
Frame
Deep channel section with cruciform bracing.

Suspension
Semi-elliptical rear springs, independent open helical front springs in combination with wishbone arms on hydraulic shock absorbers. Anti-roll torsion bar at front.

Shock absorbers
Hydraulic double-acting lever arm shock absorbers at rear with variable pressure-pump driven from gearbox, controlled by lever on steering column.

Brakes
Mechanical at rear, hydraulic at front, internal expanding pedal operated assisted by mechanical friction disc servo. Brake reaction on front suspension taken by torque arms. Finned brake drums 12¼in (317.5mm) diameter by 2¼in (57.15mm) wide Ferodo VG91 linings. Handbrake handle mounted on scuttle operated on rear wheels only.

Steering
Cam and roller with divided track rod ratio 12.25:1.

Chassis lubrication
One-shot pedal-operated chassis lubrication system with 2 pint (1.14 litres) capacity tank on bulkhead.

Top left: Offside view of Mark VI engine.

Left middle: Near side view.

Below: Works view of Mark VI chassis.

Exhaust system

Two-piece manifold, two silencers and single tailpipe. Later cars, twin system with four silencers and two tailpipes.

Wheels

Pressed-steel disc type 5in x 16in (127mm x 406mm) well-base with balance weight and covering wheel discs. Five left-hand or right-hand threaded fixing nuts.

Tyres

India Super Silent rayon 6.50in x 16in (165.1mm x 406.4mm).

PRINCIPAL CHASSIS DETAILS AND DIMENSIONS

Wheelbase: 10ft (3.05m).
Track: Front 4ft 8¾in (1.44m); Rear 4ft 10⅝in (1.49m).
Overall length: 16ft (4.88m), Wilmot Breedon type bumpers.
16ft 4¼in (4.99m) Pyrene type bumpers.
Overall body width: 5ft 11in (1.80m).
Turning circle: Right 46ft 5in (14.15m); Left 44ft 11in (13.69m).
Ground clearance: 7¼in (184mm).
Weight: Chassis 24.46cwt (1,242.8kg).
With standard steel body: 37.59cwt (1,909.5kg).

Performance: Maximum speed: 4¼-litre 94mph (151.25km/h).
4½-litre 102.3mph (164.6km/h).
Petrol consumption 18-20mpg.
Price at introduction: Chassis £1,785 (excluding purchase tax).
Standard steel saloon £2,997 (including £652 purchase tax).
Number built: 4¼-litre 4,000
4½-litre 1,201
Radiator badge: Black enamel background and winged 'B' mascot on radiator.

Two catalogue illustrations:

Below: A two-door sports saloon by James Young Ltd. Seating five, including the driver, the car has adjustable bucket-type front seats. A special feature is the ventilation system, which is controllable from the front seat.

Bottom: A drop-head foursome coupé by Park Ward Ltd on a Mark VI chassis. The folding head is power operated and is specially designed to enhance the appearance of the car when open, making it an ideal dual-purpose vehicle.

Mark VI KXH935

Chassis No: I311 EW   Engine No: B256 E

Of all the early post-World War II Bentleys the Park Ward four-seater drop-head on the Mark VI chassis must be one of the most elegant. KXH 935 was supplied new by Jack Barclay Ltd of London to Sir Robert McAlpine. Mr J. Elvins of Worcestershire, England, is the fourth owner, having bought the car in 1964. Mr Elvins uses the car for normal commuting and touring. To date the car has covered nearly 300,000 miles (482,700km).

Mark VI AH1111

Chassis No: B42AK   Engine No: B37A   Registered: 1947

This is a rather special foursome drop-head coupé by H.J. Mulliner Ltd built specially for the Maharajah Gaekwar of Baroda in 1947. Chassis No B42AK, engine No B37A. This car is now owned by Mr G. Milligen of Norfolk, England.

Mark VI Special AEK50

Two young Bentley enthusiasts David Simpson and Charles Teal who live in Warwickshire, England, decided to build a pair of 'specials' using parts from run-down Mark VIs. The two cars were built up side by side and are almost identical. AEK 50 which is David Simpson's car is used for normal pleasure motoring, while Charles Teal uses his for competition work and is seen (right) on the starting grid at the Bentley Drivers Club meeting at Silverstone in 1977.

R-Type & R-Type Continental

In June 1952 the R-Type was presented to the public and it owed its name to the fact that the VI series had by this time reached the chassis letter R.

The standard four-door, four-light saloon was very similar in nearly all respects to the Mark VI that it replaced. Externally the principal point of recognition was the obviously longer boot, which had a large one-piece lid made of aluminium. The rear wings also dispensed with the previously fitted wheelspats, and shapely mudguards flowed out of the main body shell, increasing the length of the body by $7\frac{1}{2}$in (190.50mm). The rear of the chassis was extended by the same amount, and the chassis was now of all-welded construction, not riveted as had been the Mark VI. Some detail changes to the specification were made, including automatic choke, and two-speed windscreen wipers, together with an electric de-mister for the rear window. More dual colour coachwork options were introduced, the body lines lending themselves handsomely to such treatment.

In October 1952, automatic transmission became a factory option, a General Motors Hydra-matic design being used. It had two primary epicyclic gear trains, four forward speeds and reverse, with a fluid coupling; later in 1954 the automatic transmission became standard, incorporating many refinements introduced by Rolls-Royce. To give increased sharpness to the radiator shell an extra central bar was fitted towards the end of the series.

The only petrol available in 1952 was the dreadful 'Pool', rated at 74 octane. The 93 grade which was available in 1953 offered opportunities for increased compression ratios and later cars took advantage of this. In December 1951, a standard $4\frac{1}{2}$-litre R-type was road-tested by *Autocar* and it recorded a best speed of 100mph (160km/h) together with acceleration from 0 to 50mph (0 to 80km/h) of 10.2 sec; no mean effort for a saloon car weighing $36\frac{1}{2}$cwts, (1,854kg) unladen!

The compact R-Type saloon became one of the most popular Bentleys built, More were sold each year, in the three years of its production, than any other since the first of the new breed appeared in 1933, 2,528 R-Type chassis were built (including 208 Continentals). A total of about half of the full production achieved on the Mark VI range during its six-year run.

Below: A Standard 'R'-type chassis No B344NZ with engine No B172N fitted with Park Ward drop-head coachwork. Registered 1952.

Facing page: 'R' type standard steel saloon, chassis No B106ZY, engine No B178Z, fitted with General Motors hydra-matic automatic transmission, photographed when owned by J. H. L. Adams.

In 1952 the R-Type Continental was introduced, the original conception of which was a light alloy, two-door sports saloon body, aerodynamically styled, fitted to an R-Type chassis with a tuned 4,566cc engine, and benefiting from a special exhaust system, which alone gave a further 25bhp, and a delightful hubble-bubble exhaust note. The final design incorporated a large wrap-around wind-screen, a sharply sloped rear roof-line, slight rear wing fins to give stability in side winds and rear wheelspats. The radiator was lower by 1½in (38.1mm), and in the prototype there were alloy window frames and bumpers, (changed however on the production cars). The seat frames were also built of alloy tubing. The insistence on weight-saving was influenced to no small degree by the weight that the tyres then available could carry at 100mph plus (160km/h), and the first production body weighed only 6½cwt (330.5kg). A radio was included in the price, but in efforts to save weight was only fitted if requested by the owner! While in the prototype stage, the car was known at the works as the Corniche II, but it was intro-duced to the public as the 'A' Continental.

In 1947 Walter Steator, the Rolls-Royce agent in Paris, com-missioned the design and construction by Pinin Farina of a 'fast

back' coachbuilt body mounted on a Mark VI chassis, and named the 'Cresta'. This car was shown at the 1947 Paris Salon and later produced in limited numbers by Facel Metalon, and may well have influenced the shape of the Continental. Several of the 'Cresta's' chassis modifications were incorporated by the factory in their prototype car.

The body style that resulted was very similar to the flow-free and airline saloons which had been built in the thirties. H.J. Mulliner of Chiswick built 193 bodies of this classic style, and followed the fast-back lines of the prototype car. Park Ward, Franay, Graber and Farina built another 15 cars of differing body styles. A 116.9mph (188.1km/h) maximum speed achieved by the prototype, made the Continental the fastest production four-seater in the world at the time – real performance once more back with the Bentley name. Its selling price in 1952 was £7,608 and it was eagerly sought by those attracted to a car with high performance and fine styling together with the desirable specification offered by this new breed of Bentley. The model was introduced initially for export only, and 100 of the cars went abroad. At the end of 1952 it

became available on the home market.

The engine could be run up to 4,250 rpm which gave a road speed of 116.9mph (188.1km/h) in top gear; the axle had a high final drive ratio coupled with a close-ratio gearbox, all at a weight of about 33cwts (1,678kg) in the early cars. Subsequent luxurious body and trimming requirements increased this somewhat, but the model also benefited from extensive Continental road-testing and development, which culminated with a 4,887cc engine being fitted in July 1954, this being the final development of the straight six-cylinder engine. The normal manual gear-change was on the right-hand side but a central gear-change, devised for the export market, was fitted to three of the cars released on the home market. Halfway through the production run automatic transmission was offered, but only 43 were ordered by customers.

With a thoroughness that is a special feature of its makers, the Continental handbook had kilometres-miles conversion charts shown, similarly pounds-kilos per square centimetre were also given for tyre pressures; the car was literally designed for the Continent.

Left: R-Type Continental chassis No BC31C, engine No BCC30 body by H.J. Mulliner Ltd at one time owned by Mr R.S. Pulvertaft of Yorkshire, England.

Above: Front and back views of another Mulliner-bodied Continental chassis No BC18B, engine No BCB17 owned by Mr R.S. Liebman of the USA.

Behind the development of this car was H.I.F. Evernden MBE, BSc, one of an enthusiastic team that helped to design the Mk V Corniche, and many lessons learned then were given due regard when the R-Type Continental was conceived. In his position as Chief Project Engineer of the Motor Car Division of Rolls-Royce, he was largely responsible for its design, with Chief Stylist J.P. Blatchley looking after the body styling.

This model, one of the finest produced rejoicing in the name of Bentley, has become a classic. Only 208 chassis were produced between 1952 and 1955, each chassis number prefixed by the additional letter C, to give a BC series, and this C prefix was carried by all subsequent Continentals.

197

SPECIFICATION

R-TYPE

In production 1952-55.

Basic specification at introduction as for Mark VI 4½-litres except as follows:

ENGINE
Compression ratio 6.4:1; later 6.75:1

Lubrication
1951 M series and onwards full flow Vokes oil filter.

Carburettors
Twin SU type H6 fully automatic choke.

Instruments
Electrically wound clock instead of mechanical.

TRANSMISSION
Gearbox
Manual as for 4½-litres Mark VI, automatic epicyclic gears and torque converter with kick-down change and over-ride control lever on steering column.

 Automatic ratio: Reverse, 4.3:1; First, 3.82:1; Second, 2.63:1; Third, 1.45:1; Top, direct.
 Manual close ratio: Reverse, 2.8:1; First, 2.7:1; Second, 1.82:1; Third, 1.22:1; Top, direct.
 Oil capacity: Automatic 20 pints (11.37 litres), manual 6 pints (3.41 litres).

Rear axle and final drive
As for 4½-litres Mark VI, early models giving engine to road wheel ratio in top of 11/41 (3.727:1). Later cars had 12/41 (3.42:1).
 Oil capacity 1¾ pints (0.995 litres).

CHASSIS
Frame
As for Mark VI but, later, weld joints replaced riveted construction.

Brakes
Basically as for Mark VI except for slight increase in brake friction area.

Autocar

Windscreen wipers
Late cars fitted with Trico vacuum-operated windscreen washers.

PRINCIPAL CHASSIS DETAILS AND DIMENSIONS
Overall length: 16ft 7½in (5.073m) with Wilmot Breedon bumpers.
 16ft 11½in (5.169m) with Pyrene bumpers.
Overall body width: 5ft 7½in (1.715m).
Performance: Maximum speed 106.5mph (171.35km/h).
 Petrol consumption: Manual 18-20mpg; Automatic 16-18mpg.
Price at introduction: Chassis £2,270 (excluding purchase tax).
 Standard steel saloon £4,824 (including £1,724 purchase tax).

Number built: 2,320.

Below: A Canadian-registered Continental AXF304 Toronto. chassis No BC4D, engine No BCD4, owned by Mr G. Minden.

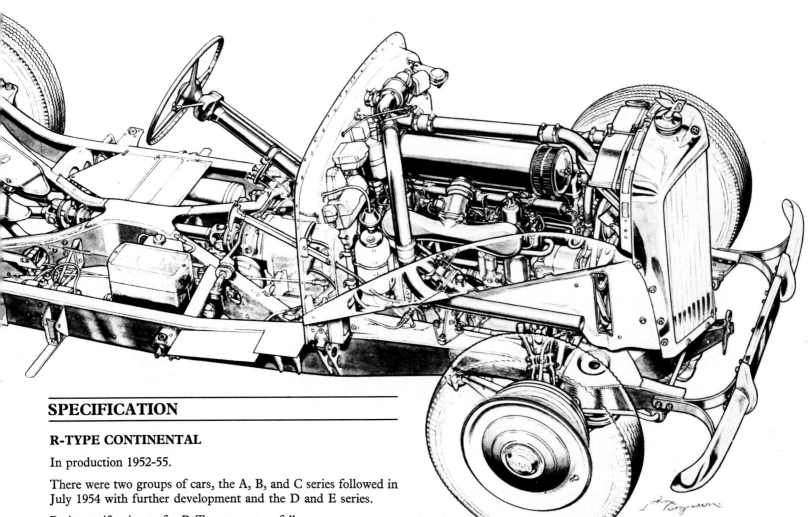

SPECIFICATION

R-TYPE CONTINENTAL

In production 1952-55.

There were two groups of cars, the A, B, and C series followed in July 1954 with further development and the D and E series.

Basic specification as for R-Type except as follows:

ENGINE
6 cylinder; firing order 1, 4, 2, 6, 3, 5 (maximum safe rpm 4,250).

	A, B, C series	D, E series
Bore	3⅝in (92mm)	3.725in (95mm)
Stroke	4½in (1,143mm)	4½in (1,143mm)
Cubic capacity	4,566cc (278.6cu in)	4,887cc (298.2cu in)
Compression ratio	7.0:1; 7.20:1; 7.25:1	7.25:1
Brake horsepower	137 (approximately)	Not available
RAC rating	31½hp	33.7hp

Crankshaft
Main journals 2.75in (70mm) diameter and crankpins 2in (50.8mm) diameter.

Carburettors
Twin SU type HD8 2in (50.8mm) mostly with automatic choke, except chassis BC2LA to BC60LA.

Instruments
A revolution counter was fitted.

TRANSMISSION
Gearbox
Four forward speeds and reverse. Synchromesh on second, third and top. Right-hand gate change. Automatic gearbox (from D series).

Ratios: Manual, Reverse, 2.861:1; First, 2.67:1; Second, 1.54:1; Third, 1.21:1; Top, direct.
Automatic, Reverse, 4.3:1; First, 3.82:1; Second, 2.63:1; Third, 1.45:1; Top, direct.
Oil capacity: Manual, 6 pints (3.41 litres).
Automatic, 20 pints (11.37 litres).

Above: 'Autocar' chassis drawing by John Ferguson.

Rear axle and final drive
As for R-Type, but giving engine to road wheel ratio in top of 14/40 (3.077:1).

CHASSIS
Exhaust system
Two-piece manifold to single large-bore pipe, with two large silencer boxes and single tailpipe.

Tyres
6.50in x 16in (165mm x 406mm) India Speed Special.

PRINCIPAL CHASSIS DETAILS AND DIMENSIONS
Wheelbase: 10ft (3.048m).
Track: Front 4ft 8½in (1.435m); Rear 4ft 10½in (1,486m).
Overall length: 17ft 2½in (5.245m).
17ft 7½in (5.372m) with export bumpers.
Overall body width: 5ft 11½in (1.816m).
Turning circle: 43ft (13.106m).
Ground clearance: 7in (178mm).
Weight: 24½cwt (1,234.8kg).
With H. J. Mulliner sports saloon 32¼cwt (1,625.4kg).
Performance: Maximum speed (116.9mph) 188.09km/h).
Petrol consumption 20-21mpg.
Price at introduction: Chassis £2,440 (excluding purchase tax).
With H. J. Mulliner sport saloon £6,512
(including £2,327 purchase tax).
Number built: 208.

R-Type Continental OLG490

Chassis No: BC26A   **Engine No: BH11**   **Registered: 1951**

This car, which was the prototype 'R' Continental and was used by Rolls-Royce Ltd as the demonstration car, has been described many times in the motoring press but not in more glowing terms than by Raymond Mays in the 'Autocar'. In a 1952 'Autocar' road report the car was described as 'A Modern Magic Carpet'. In 1961 Rolls-Royce sold the car, after a certain amount of persuasion and a complete overhaul, to Mr Stanley Sedgwick who is still her proud owner. Before the car was handed over the chassis number was changed from 9B6 to BC26A. Since Stanley Sedgwick has owned the car it has completed many Continental journeys at high average speeds including a journey in September 1970 from Eze-Sur-Me between Nice and Monte Carlo to Surrey, a distance of 847.3 miles (1,363.3km), in 17 hours 55 minutes including a Channel crossing by sea. The journey from Eze-Sur-Mer to Boulogne, a distance of 752.3 miles (1,210.45km) had been covered in a running time of 12 hours 10 minutes – an average speed of 61.08mph (98.29km/h): truly Continental motoring. OLG 490 is pictured below on the Route Napoleon, France, in 1961.

R-Type Continental HRX990

Chassis No: BC9B   **Engine No: BCB9**   **Registered: July 1953**

Another much-travelled Continental is that of Mr Michael Collier of Berkshire, England, who has taken his car to most countries in Europe and written of his journeys in the 'Autocar' and other publications. HRX 990 has now covered well over 250,000 miles (402,250km). The two pictures below show the car in Spain.

R-Type Continental OUK999

Chassis No: BC49C   Engine No: BCC48   Registered: June 1955

OUK999 is an interesting car as it is the only 'R'-type Continental chassis fitted with a two-seater fixed-head body specially designed and constructed by Pinin Farina. When supplied new this car cost £6,929 inclusive of purchase tax. In August 1965 it was the subject of an article in the 'Autocar' No 242 in the series 'Used Cars on the Road'. It was then for sale, the asking price being £2,750. Later in 1965 it was bought by Mr J.B. Broadway of Worcester-shire, England, who still owns the car. It is interesting to note that on the 'Autocar' test in 1965 the car would still reach 90mph (144.81km/h) from a standing start in thirty-one seconds. To date the car has covered about 37,000 miles (59,533km) from new. As can be seen in the picture on the right, this is one of the very few Bentleys with a central gear shift lever – no doubt to make it easier for the driver to get in and out of the car.

S-Type & S-Continental

April 1955 saw the advent of the S-Type four-door, four-light saloon, commonly known as the S1, to distinguish it from succeeding models in the same series. It was an entirely different car from its predecessors, being longer and wider, with a stronger chassis, fitted with four-wheel hydraulic brakes, but it utilised a modified late R-Type 4.9-litre Continental engine, fitted with an automatic choke. It was given better cylinder-head porting, but only equipped with a single-pipe exhaust system. The inlet port modifications almost followed vintage practice, in that half of the manifold was cut into the cylinder head, but there it fed into six separate ports. Produced as standard with an automatic transmission, a manual gearbox and power steering were optional extras. The automatic gearbox was the original General Motors type, with hydraulic coupling, manufactured by Rolls-Royce under licence, and it incorporated a kick-down change enabling the driver to hold the low and intermediate gears. The variable ride control was electrically operated. For the first time since 1933, a radiator cap was not fixed to the top of the radiator shell, a slim winged 'B' occupying a position of solitary splendour!

The body was produced by Pressed Steel Ltd, in an all-steel stressed-skin form, on a wheelbase increased to 10ft 3in (3.12m); a longer version at 10ft 7in (3.22m) was also available. The interior of the body had wide and luxurious seats, upholstered in English hide, giving ample room for five or six people, and a commodious boot could take five or six average-size suitcases. The seats had folding centre armrests, front and rear, and vanity mirrors, cigar lighters and picnic trays were, of course, standard equipment.

The huge chassis was of a closed box-section welded-steel construction with cruciform centre bracing pierced for the propeller shaft, the whole forming a very stiff frame. Independent front suspension was by wishbones of unequal length, with coil springs. Conventional half-elliptic rear springs operating in rubber-bushed shackles were utilised; the whole was carried on broad-based tyres.

Below: A Frank Wootton painting of the S1 Bentley.

Two position ride control was fitted to the rear shock absorbers, as was normal practice with the marque. It was the beginning of what was to be a never-ending increase in the detailed specification of the cars, an example being the interior car heater which had summer and winter matrix settings, to give a carefully controlled influx of heat. Power-assisted steering was in such demand that fifty chassis, in the midst of having bodies fitted, had power-steering conversions adapted to them, and in October 1956 it became a standard factory fitting.

To quote the then current sales brochure, 'The latest marque of the famous Bentley motor car is the S Series. It has a luxury saloon body, and a performance which combines superlative acceleration to a speed of more than 100mph (160km/h) with smooth silent running and powerful, sensitive brakes.' The car was almost the size of a limousine, although the limousines that were built generally used the 10ft 7in (3.22m) wheelbase. *Autocar* found during road-tests made in October 1955, that the car was capable of covering the standing ¼ mile (400m) in 18.9sec. with acceleration through the gears of 0 to 60mph (96.54km/h) in 14.2 seconds.

As well as the standard four-door saloon, several types of specialist bodywork were built on the chassis, 157 receiving bodies from craftsmen and designers employed by James Young, Hooper, Freestone and Webb, Graber and H.J. Mulliner. The left-hand-drive version of the car proved more popular than with the VI and R-Types, 690 being exported. The car was particularly acceptable in the USA, also many went to Australia, France and Switzerland. A total of over 3,000 cars were built up to the end of 1960, by which time its successor had been announced.

Below: S1 Continental 594 KEA, chassis No BC6EL, engine No BC6E, photographed at Stratford-upon-Avon, England, in 1969. This is now owned by Mr J.J. Pennington of Cheshire, England, and bears the registration No TNA 1.

The success of the first Continental ensured that a sporting version would obviously be offered as part of the S-Type range, and a model was shown some six months after the introduction of the standard saloon. It was based on the previous high-performance chassis, having a high-compression engine, mounted under a low bonnet line, with a radiator slightly contoured forward, high axle ratio and tyre equipment specifically designed to give less rolling resistance. Performance equalled or bettered that of the early R-Type Continentals, its maximum speed and acceleration were impressive, 0 to 80mph in 21.3 secs (0 to 128.72km/h), and a best speed of about 120mph (193.08km/h) from its 4.9 litre (298.3cc) engine. Once again real Bentley performance.

Most cars were built with the standard automatic transmission, but a few synchromesh gearboxes were produced to special order until 1957, being offered as an optional extra. Later cars, probably influenced by the higher octane petrol available, had an even higher compression cylinder head, together with larger inlet valves; all cars had a special felt air-cleaner fitted. H.J. Mulliner retained their familiar fast back body style which had benefited from wind-tunnel testing for many of the 218 bodies that they built on the Continental chassis, but introduced scalloping into the rear mudguards and at the same time dispensed with the wheelspats. Park Ward of Chiswick was the only other major coachbuilder, involved with a further 185 cars offering fixed and drophead two-door bodies. A further 28 bodies were fitted by James Young, Hooper Graber and Franay, making a total of 431 S1 Continentals in all.

In May 1957 the 'Flying Spur' made its debut. It was a special four-door saloon built by H.J. Mulliner, on the Continental chassis, to incorporate the essential features suggested by that name, that is lightness, low wind resistance, and an emphasis on high performance. It was a splendid car with delightful lines, and the first one to carry this famous name was constructed on chassis number BC 90BT, and its construction took five months commencing December 1956.

SPECIFICATION

S1-TYPE (Standard and long wheelbase)

In production: Standard 1955-59.
Long wheelbase 1957-59.

Basic specification at introduction (with some production modifications):

ENGINE
6 cylinders; firing order 1, 4, 2, 6, 3, 5.

Bore	3¾in (95.25mm)
Stroke	4½in (114.3mm)
Cubic capacity	4,887cc (298.2 cu in).
Compression ratio	6.6:1 and (later cars) 8.0:1.
Brake horsepower	178 (approximate).
RAC rating	33.7hp

Valves
As Mark VI and R-Type.

Cylinder block and pistons
Monobloc cast-iron, full-length cylinder liners, aluminium pistons with top ring chromium-plated.

Crankcase and sump
As Mark VI and R-Type.

Crankshaft
As R-Type but cone plugs to crankshaft made of stainless steel.

Lubrication
As R-Type.

Ignition
Coil (Lucas or Delco Remy) and Delco Remy distributor. Octane adjuster, calibrated slide fitted to distributor. Automatic advance and retard. One sparking plug per cylinder (Lodge HLNP or Champion) N5 14mm.

Carburettors
Twin SU HD6 1¾in (44.5mm), later HD8 2in (50.8mm). Automatic control for starting by separate solenoid in ignition circuit.

Dynamo
Lucas (special equipment) Model C47, 12 volt automatic regulation of output, to 57amp hour battery.

Above: S1 Continental drophead coupé by Park Ward.

Facing page: S1 Continental Sport Saloon by Park Ward.

Starter
Lucas (special equipment) Model M45G with planetary reduction gear.

Instruments
Fuel/oil level gauge, speedometer, ammeter, oil pressure gauge, water temperature gauge, clock.

Cooling system
Centrifugal water-pump and five-bladed fan. Thermostatically controlled. Water capacity 28 pints (15.93 litres).

Petrol system
Twin SU pumps of special alloy construction fitted to off side of the centre section of chassis. Rear petrol tank of 18 gallon (29.58 litres) capacity.

TRANSMISSION
Gearbox
Four-speed automatic epicyclic gears and fluid flywheel with kick-down change and steering column control. Manual synchromesh gearbox available to special order (only about ten cars fitted).
Ratios: Automatic; Reverse, 4.3:1; First, 3.82:1; Second, 2:63:1; Third, 1.45:1; Top, direct.
Close Ratio Manual: Reverse, 2.86:1; First, 2.67:1; Second, 1.55:1; Third, 1.22:1; Top, direct.
Oil capacity: Automatic 20 pints (11.38 litres); Manual 6 pints (11.37 litres).

Clutch
Manual only: 11in (279mm) single dry plate.

Propeller shaft
Open divided shaft with flexibly mounted centre bearing.

Rear axle and final drive
Semi-floating type, hypoid bevel with four-pinion differential giving engine to road wheel ratio in top of 12/41 (3.42:1).
Oil capacity 1½ pints (0.85 litres).

CHASSIS
Frame
Closed box-section of 16-gauge welded steel with cruciform centre

bracing. Steel front pan carrying suspension and steering. Tubular cross-member at rear.

Suspension
Independent front suspension by unequal length wishbones and helical coil springs. Rear suspension by half-elliptic springs with rubber bushed shackles. Anti-roll bars at front and 'Z' bar fitted to rear axle.

Shock absorbers
Rolls-Royce opposed piston hydraulic dampers at front. Electrical ride controlled piston type dampers at rear, two-position ride control switch on steering column.

Brakes
Friction disc type servo-assisted self-adjusting type with hydraulic operation at front, hydraulic and mechanical operation at the rear. Dual master cylinders. Pull and twist scuttle-mounted handbrake acting on rear wheels only. 11¼in (286mm) diameter cast-iron drums 3in (76mm) wide with peripheral cooling fins.

Steering
Early cars manual was standard, later cars had power steering as standard. Cam and roller type to three-piece track linkage. Ratio: manual 20.6:1; power 18.7:1. Capacity of power steering system 4 pints (2.275 litres).

Chassis lubrication
Centralised pressure lubrication system fed by reservoir on scuttle operated by foot pedal.

Exhaust system
Two-piece manifold, twin down-pipes joining single pipe to single silencer, two resonators and single tailpipe.

Wheels
Steel, well-base rims, secured with five nuts left- and right-hand threads, 6in x 15in (152 x 381mm).

Tyres
8.20in x 15in (208mm x 381mm).

PRINCIPAL CHASSIS DETAILS AND DIMENSIONS
Wheelbase: Standard 10ft 3in (3.124m); Long 10ft 7in (3.226m).
Track: Front 4ft 10in (1.473m); Rear 5ft (1.524m).
Overall length: 17ft 8in (5.385m); long wheelbase 17ft 11¾in (5.48m).
Overall body width: 6ft 2¾in (1.899m).

Turning circle: Right and left 41ft 8in (12.7m).
Ground clearance: 7in (178mm).
Weight: Standard chassis 25.92cwt (1,306.37kg).
Standard body 40cwt (2,016kg).
Performance: Maximum speed: 6.6:1 compression 101mph (162.51km/h). 8.0:1 compression 106mph (170.55km/h).
Petrol consumption: 15-16mpg.
Price at introduction: Standard chassis £2,465 (excluding purchase tax).
Standard saloon manual gearbox £4,669 (including £1,374 purchase tax).
Automatic gearbox was £99.3.4 extra (including £29.3.4 purchase tax).
Long wheelbase saloon £6,894 (including £2,299 purchase tax).
Radio: Radiomobile 200X 7-valve radio was standard equipment.
Number built: 3,072 plus thirty-five long wheelbase cars.

S1-TYPE CONTINENTAL

In production 1955-59.

All details as for standard chassis S-Type except as listed.

ENGINE
Compression ratios 7.25:1 and 8.0:1.

TRANSMISSION
Rear axle and final drive
Engine to road wheel ratio in top of 13/38 (2.92:1) or 13/40 (3.077:1).

Tyres
7.60in x 15in (193mm x 381mm) or 8in x 15in (203mm x 381mm).

PRINCIPAL CHASSIS DETAILS AND DIMENSIONS
Overall body width: 5ft 11½in (1.82m).
Weight: Chassis 25.24cwt (1,272.1kg).
With H. J. Mulliner body 33½cwt (1,688kg).
Performance: Maximum speed 120½mph (193.88km/h).
Petrol consumption 17-18mpg.
Price at introduction: Chasis £2,510 (excluding purchase tax).
H. J. Mulliner sports saloon £7,028 (including £2,068 purchase tax).

Number built: 431.

S2 & S3 & Continentals

In August 1959 the factory introduced the S2, and stand 137 at the October Motor Show revealed the significant mechanical changes that had been made. It was later also exhibited at the company's Paris showrooms on the avenue Kleber. The previously used automatic gearbox was now the only transmission available, and the car was fitted with a new V8 engine, which used an alloy cylinder block and cylinder heads. Developed over a period of five years, it was an over-square 90° Vee unit of 6,230cc with hydraulic tappets operating the overhead valves. The considerable amount of cast alloy used in its construction enabled it to be the same weight as the Straight Six that it superseded, and of course there was a considerable increase in the power available, although as usual the factory declined to quote actual brake horsepower, stating that it was 'sufficient'! This is really because it is very difficult to give meaningful comparative bhp figures. At the same time a higher axle ratio was introduced. This specification gave the car a genuine top speed of over 110mph (177km/h) with acceleration from 0 to 60mph (0 to 96.54km/h) in 10.9 seconds; the figure was recorded by *Motor* in May 1960, in a sister car to the S2, a Rolls-Royce Silver Cloud II.

Outwardly, the body was indistinguishable from the S1, with the exception of the slight differences in the front flasher and sidelight assemblies, changed overriders, and the slightly reduced radiator height. One-shot lubrication was omitted for the first time since 1933, and was substituted by grease nipples, with long periods between servicing. Inside the car were a slimmer and smaller steering wheel and a speedometer that now read to 120mph (193km/h); air louvres were also fitted to the fascia below the windscreen. A high standard of finish was still maintained. The showroom brochure boasted 'The lovely lines of the Bentley are finished with the utmost care by the application of at least 14 coats of paint'. It was the traditional way that cars were painted in the 1920s, when a lengthy procedure was involved. About five or six foundation coats were first applied, then a layer of black paint which percolated into the undercoats which were of thin body. The

Below: A standard S3 saloon 444 HUW chassis No 6308EC, engine No BEC154, owned by Mr J. Smith of Somerset, England.

surface was then pumice-stoned until the black ceased to show, and at this point the final coats of paint would be applied. Modern techniques ensured that these hard-won standards of quality were continued.

The Continental version had a slightly higher axle ratio and special broad-base tyres were used, but it differed from the standard car in hardly any other respect, except that four-shoes-per-drum front brakes were introduced to cope with the very high speeds at which the Continentals were regularly being driven. The gap in terms of mechanical refinement, body streamlining and treatment between the saloon and the Continental had narrowed, so that there was no longer any significant difference in many instances between the two versions, although the Continental was only available with specialist coachwork.

Much coachbuilding work had been undertaken by H.J. Mulliner, and the business was purchased by Rolls-Royce in 1959, and became Mulliner Park Ward Ltd, in 1961. Mulliner and Park Ward together built around 346 bodies, and another thirty chassis enjoyed the attentions of specialists from James Young, Hooper, Graber and Franay. Mulliners also built 15 drophead coupés, a body based on the standard S2 shell supplied from Crewe. The established aesthetic line of the marque was continued in all these cars, the practice of supplying a chassis with a fixed height bulkhead and dashboard helping to ensure that basic design lines were unaltered.

The standard S2 with its improved performance soon became only second to the R-Type in numbers produced annually – an average of over 900 cars per year leaving the factory between August 1959 and May 1962, plus 577 left-hand-drive models reflecting its continued high standing in the world markets.

The S3 made its debut at the Motor Show in October 1962, only differing from the S2 outwardly by its four (Lucas $5\frac{3}{4}$in dia. sealed beam units) main head-light system, and the smaller bumper over-riders. However, engine compression and carburation modifications had increased the power by about five to seven per cent, delivered through a standard automatic transmission. The exhaust system had three acoustic silencers made of stainless steel, each tuned in series to absorb a different range of frequencies, so that 'only the ticking of the clock could be heard'!

Many detail refinements were added and the tradition of superb craftsmanship was shown in its finish, from the beautiful leather upholstery to the fascia and garnish rails finished in French Walnut veneer; power lift windows, tinted glass, fitted suitcases for the boot and refrigerated air-conditioning were optional extras; a headlight flasher button was also incorporated in the direction indicator lever. Passenger comfort had increased with more leg room and seat width provided in the rear. To achieve the standard of silence required, insulation was installed at every possible point of vibration; in fact the brochure proudly quoted that 'the only point of direct connection between the body and the chassis is the speedometer cable'!

The S3 Continental chassis was for the first time identical to the standard one. The reputation that the first R-Type Continental had achieved, of being accepted as a true sports saloon, had changed, and the cars had virtually assumed the status and appearance of the traditional Rolls-Royce saloon car of the pre- and post-war years. In other words the Bentley had truly lost its individual identity. However both versions of the S3 had a 110mph plus (177km/h) performance.

When the last S3 Continental was sold on the 31 January 1966, 7,478 S-Type chassis, with standard and specialist coachwork had been delivered, including 1,131 completed as Continental versions. Volume production in terms of the 'standard' steel body completed at Crewe monopolised the post-war Bentley scene. No less than 12,379 'standard' bodies were produced, out of a grand total of 15,207 cars, from VI to S3 inclusive. Of the coachbuilt cars, H.J. Mulliner (owned by Rolls-Royce from 1959) built 1,127 cars, and Park Ward (owned since 1939 by Rolls-Royce) constructed 682. Of other private coachbuilders still in business James Young, Hooper and Freestone and Webb, built 823 between them; the rest of the chassis, some 296, were clad with bodies by a further 33 other coachbuilders. Thus the number of bodybuilding specialists had reduced from 119 in the 1920s, down to 38 post-war survivors actually building bodies for the Bentley motor car. Several companies had withdrawn from the type of work involved, but the others had disappeared.

SPECIFICATION

S2-TYPE (Standard, long wheelbase and Continental).

In production 1959-62.

Basic specification at introduction (with some production modifications):

ENGINE

8 cylinders in 'V' formation; 'A' bank off side; 'B' bank near side; firing order A1, B1, A4, B4, B2, A3, B3, A2

Bore	4.1in (104.14mm)
Stroke	3.6in (9.44mm)
Cubic capacity	6,230cc (380.2cu in).
Compression ratio	8.0:1
Brake horsepower	not disclosed

Valves and camshaft
Two valves per cylinder, overhead operated by push-rods and rockers from central camshaft. Self-adjusting hydraulic tappets.

Cylinder block and crankcase
High silicon content cast-aluminium-alloy in 90° 'V' form with 'wet' cast-iron cylinder liners. Detachable alloy cylinder heads with Austerite steel valve seats. Single-piece sump pan.

Crankshaft
Nitrided chrome molybdenum steel with integral balance weights, running in five main bearings. Crankshaft damper.

Lubrication
Oil pump, full-flow filter, pressure feed to crankshaft, con-rods, camshaft and hydraulic tappets. Sump capacity $12\frac{1}{2}$ pints (7.1 litres).

Ignition
Coil, Delco Remy or Lucas. Later models had vacuum and centrifugal advance and retard mechanism. Sparking plugs one per cylinder, Lodge CLNP or Champion RN8 14mm.

Carburettors
Twin SU HD6 $1\frac{3}{4}$in (44mm) with automatic choke.

Dynamo
Lucas (special equipment) 12 volt Model C48 with current voltage regulator to 67 amp hour battery.

Starter
Lucas (special equipment) Model M45G with pre-engagement solenoid fitted.

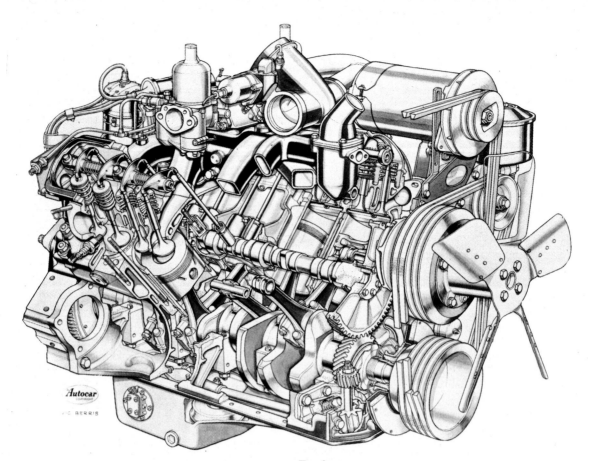

Instruments

Speedometer, clock, ammeter, water temperature gauge, fuel level gauge. (Revolution counter on Continental.)

Cooling system

Centrifugal pump mounted in tandem with fan, belt-driven. Water capacity 21 pints (11.944 litres).

Petrol system

Twin independent SU electric pumps fitted externally on frame from 18 gallon (81.9 litres) tank.

TRANSMISSION

Gearbox

Rolls-Royce automatic gearbox with four forward speeds and reverse through epicyclic gears. Kick-down change and steering column control lever.

> Ratios: Reverse, 4.3:1; First, 3.82:1; Second, 2.63:1; Third, 1.45:1; Top, direct.
> Oil capacity 20 pints (11.375 litres).

Propeller shaft

Open type divided into two connected by three universal joints.

Rear axle and final drive

Semi-floating hypoid bevel with four-star differential giving engine to road wheel ratio in top. Standard and long wheelbase, 13/40 (3.08:1); Continental 13/38 (2.92:1).

> Oil capacity 1½ pints (0.853 litres).

CHASSIS

Frame

Closed box-section frame of welded steel construction with cruciform centre bracing.

Suspension

A S-Type.

Shock absorbers

As S-Type.

Brakes

Friction-disc type servo operating hydraulic front and hydraulic-mechanical rear brakes similar to S-Type. Pull and twist handbrake on rear wheels. The Continental had four shoes on each front wheel.

Chassis lubrication

Twenty-one long-life grease points.

Exhaust system

Twin manifolds feeding to single large-diameter pipe, three acoustic silencers and single tailpipe.

Wheels

As for S-Type.

Tyres

Dunlop 8.20in x 15in (208mm x 381mm).
Continental: Dunlop broad base 8in x 15in (203mm x 381mm).

PRINCIPAL CHASSIS DETAILS AND DIMENSIONS – S2 ONLY

	Standard Saloon	Two-door Continental
Wheelbase:	10ft 3in (3.12m); lwb 10ft 7in (3.23m)	10ft 3in (3.12m)
Track:		
Front	4ft 10½in (1.49m)	4ft 10½in (1.49m)
Rear	5ft (1.52m)	5ft (1.52m)
Overall length:	17ft 7¾in (5.38m) lwb 17ft 11¾in (5.48m)	17ft 8in (5.385m)
Overall body width:	6ft 2¾in (1.90m)	5ft 11¾in (1.82m)
Turning circle:		
Standard	41ft 8in (12.7m)	41ft 8in (12.7m)
Long wheelbase	43ft (13.3m)	43ft (13.3m)
Ground clearance:	7in (17.8mm)	7in (17.8mm)

Weight:

Chassis	26.33cwt (1,327.5kg)	26.33cwt (1,327.5kg)
With standard saloon	41.2cwt (2,076kg)	38cwt (1,915kg)

Performance:

Maximum speed	113.9mph (183.km/h)	114.5mph (184.23km/h)
Fuel consumption	14-15mpg	16-17mpg

Price at introduction:

Chassis (Standard)	£2,890 (excluding purchase tax)	£2,935 (excluding purchase tax)
Complete car	Standard £5,660 (including £1,665 purchase tax)	£8,119 (including £2,389 purchase tax)

Number built: 1,865, plus 57 long wheelbase — 388

Radiomobile 401T transistorised and five valve fitted as standard equipment.

PRINCIPAL CHASSIS DETAILS AND DIMENSIONS – S3 ONLY

	Standard Saloon and long wheelbase	Continental
Wheelbase:		
Standard	10ft 3in (3.12m)	10ft 3in (3.12m)
Long wheelbase	10ft 7in (3.23m)	
Track:		
Front	4ft 10in (1.47m)	4ft 10in (1.47m)
Rear	5 ft (1.52m)	5ft (1.52m)
Overall length:		
Standard	17ft 6¼in (5.34m)	17ft 8in (5.385m)
Long wheelbase	17ft 10¼in (5.44m)	

Above: A publicity photograph of the S2.

Facing page: A Vic Berris drawing for the 'Autocar' of the S2 engine.

Overall body width:	6ft 2¾in (1.90m)	6ft 1½in (1.84m)
Turning circle:		
Standard	41ft 8in (12.7m)	41ft 8in (12.7m)
Long wheelbase	43ft (13.3m)	
Ground clearance:	7in (17.8cm)	7in (17.8cm)
Weight:		
Chassis, standard	26.46cwt (1,333.4kg)	26.46cwt (1,333.4kg)
With standard saloon	40.70cwt (2,051kg)	38cwt (1,915.2 kg)
Performance:		
Maximum speed	117mph (188.25km/h)	117mph (188.25km/h)
Fuel consumption	14-15mpg	16-17mpg
Price at introduction:		
Chassis (standard)	£3,035 (excluding purchase tax)	£3,080 (excluding purchase tax)
Complete car, standard:	£6,127 (including £1,672 purchase tax)	£8,945 (including £2,440 purchase tax)
long wheelbase:	£7,515 (including £2,050 purchase tax)	
Number built:	1,286 (plus 32 long wheelbase)	312

S3 Continental 147HJJ

Chassis No: BC78XC   **Engine No: 39LBC**

The drop-head four-seater Continental was the ultimate in the S3 series. 147 HJJ, chassis No BC78XC, engine No 39LBC, is owned by Mr G.M. Cliffe-Jones of Birmingham, England.

T-Type & Corniche

The last of the line to date, the T model, was shown at Earls Court in October 1965. The 6,230cc V8 engine (code named L-Type) from the S series was retained with slightly modified cylinder heads, but was fitted into an entirely new body of unit construction – a completely new departure for Bentley. One in fifty of all engines produced are completely stripped and examined to ensure that the precision engineering standards desired are attained; this is done before the engine is offered into a chassis/body. The standard monocoque body is made by Pressed Steel Ltd and assembled at Crewe. It is all steel with the exception of the boot lid, bonnet and doors; all these non-stress panels are of aluminium alloy. Lower body sections are made out of galvanised steel sheeting. At this time the last few coachbuilt S-types were being completed.

It could now be said that body engineering had truly arrived, if one considers the implications of ensuring that the new monocoque creation met the stringent requirements of the marque. The advent of this car also saw for the first time complete four-wheel independent self-levelling suspension and disc brakes. It had automatic transmission with the previously used four-speed box, suitably strengthened; brakes operated by a triplicated hydraulic system, (which was changed back to a duplicate line system in 1975).

A host of sophisticated engineering devices were adapted, to give a car of very advanced technical specification and no effort was spared to reduce vibration; for example, harmonic dampers were fitted to the propeller shaft and rear drive shafts. Without going into great detail, it should be noted that the engine, gearbox and rear suspension were each mounted on their own sub-frame, with the final drive unit carried on a flexibly mounted cross-member. Each car undergoes two 30 mile road-tests before delivery.

Craftsmen continued to use beautiful Circassian, Californian, Indian, Persian or Lombardy walnut for the veneers, together with traditional deep-pile Wilton carpet and leather upholstery, using eight hides to a car, and even built-in quadrophonic sound! Yet there was a hint of steel beneath its sleek exterior, and performance was really remarkable, bearing in mind that the car's kerb weight was 41.6cwt (2,067kg). In a road-test on a sister car, a Rolls-Royce Silver Shadow, in March 1967, *Autocar* reported a mean maximum speed of 115mph (185.03km/h) from the 6,230cc engine car, a standing-start quarter mile (402km) of 17.6 seconds with 0 to

Below: A catalogue illustration of the standard T-type saloon.

60mph (96.54km/h) in 10.9 seconds.

There was still a demand for coachbuilt cars. James Young built an attractive two-door sports saloon and in 1966 Mulliner Park Ward offered a two-door sports saloon and a two-door drophead convertible in 1967. However, only the Mulliner Park Ward convertible continued to be built after 1967, and was eventually replaced by the Corniche in 1971.

In 1968 Paul Frere, the well-known racing driver, road-tested a car (in Silver Shadow form), over a 2,000-mile (3,220km) three-week period from Brussels down to Turin and back. The autoroutes were often travelled at 110mph (177km/h), and the Alps were tackled with disdainful ease. 'The car really inspires confidence not only because it behaves safely but also because I know it has been properly put together and won't let me down.' Such statements are typical of the enthusiasm that is often expressed, and the confidence associated with the names Rolls-Royce and Bentley. In the same year, the General Motors three-speed automatic gearbox with torque converter was installed, manufactured by Rolls-Royce under licence; the ratio of the power assistance to the steering was improved at about the same time, giving better 'feel'. The United States Federal Safety Specification required various modifications to be made in 1969, which included recessed door and grab handles, side marker lights and larger flashing direction indicators; refrigeration also became standard equipment.

The 6.7-litre was introduced in 1970 and the final significant change, the compliant suspension, was fitted in 1972. Briefly, this was modified front suspension wishbone struts to give controlled fore and aft compliance. At the same time the front track was increased from 57.5in to 59.4in (1.461m to 1.509m). The introduction of the 6,750cc engine did not improve performance by very much, probably due to a slight increase in weight and to extra demands of engine ancillaries, together with a reduction in compression ratio to 8:1, so that lower lead-content petrol could be used. Increased flare was given to the wheel arches to accommodate wider tyres, and automatic speed control was offered as standard early in 1974. Continual improvements were made to the car. One interesting technical alteration was the Opus electronic ignition system that was fitted to the engine unit in 1975. This equipment removed the contact breaker from the distributor and substituted an electronic device, which was more efficient in all ways.

The production of the T series Bentley only took a small part of the total car production at Crewe. 2,242 were built in either standard form or coachbuilt, as Corniche drophead and saloon, between 1965 and the end of 1976/77, including a very few LWB special order. Each Bentley had a one-year warranty given for the the body and interior, and three years or 50,000 miles (80,450km) for the remainder of the car and chassis, subject to certain exclusions. This 50,000-mile (80,450km) warranty still left a similar mileage well within the life of the engine, which was designed to run for 100,000 miles (160,900km) without a major overhaul. Each engine was bench tested to the equivalent of 150 miles (241.35km) before installation, which was typical of the care that went into the building of the Bentley.

The T series was well able to satisfy any connoisseur of motoring, be he an enthusiast or practical businessman. The Bentley image had matured through the years and had moved with the times. There is little in common with a certain noisy 3-litre that burst into bellowing sound in 1919, except that the proud name of Bentley is perpetuated by the ever-present, quiet yet exuberant, winged 'B' on the radiator, a symbol of superb engineering technology, with unremitting regard for quality; a desire to safeguard standards that have never accepted anything but the very best. While the first 3-litre could be bought for about £1,225 with an open four-seater body, the T-type saloon in January 1978 was on sale at £26,740.

SPECIFICATION

T-TYPE (Standard and long wheelbase)

In production 1965-77

Basic specification at introduction (with some production modifications):

ENGINE
8 cylinders; firing order A1, B1, A4, B4, B2, A3, B3, A2.

	As introduced	Modified July 1970
Bore	4.1in (104.1mm)	4.1in (104.1mm)
Stroke	3.6in (91.4mm)	3.9in (99.1mm)
Cubic capacity	6,230cc (380cu in)	6,750cc (411.9cu in)
Compression ratio	9.0:1	8.0:1 (from October 1975)

Brake horsepower not disclosed

Valves and camshaft
As S2-Type

Cylinder blocks and crankcase
As S2-Type but with redesigned cylinder heads with larger valve ports and repositioned sparking plugs.

Crankshaft
As S2-Type.

Lubrication
Sump capacity increased to 14½ pints (8.247 litres).

Below: The demonstration works T-type at speed on a motorway.

Ignition

As S2 until October 1975 when Lucas Opus electronic ignition fitted. Sparking plugs Champion RN14Y (later N14Y).

Carburettors

Twin SU HD8 2in (50.8mm) with automatic mixture control. Later cars had thermostatically controlled air intake.

Generator

Lucas dynamo as S2 until 1969. Then CAV AC512 12 volt 45 amp alternator later increased to 55 amp to 64 amp hour battery, later 71 amp hour. Note: alternator fitted with refrigeration.

Starter

Lucas (special equipment) with pre-engagement solenoid.

Instruments

Foot-controlled dipping switch with safety circuit; warning lamps on facia for hydraulic accumulator pressure; ammeter; engine oil pressure; coolant level; fuel level; ignition and handbrake on; stop-lamp failure warning; dimming device for fuel-warning lamp; solenoid-operated fuel filler cap; radio; cigar lighter; speedometer; Lucas electric washers. Padded facia introduced 1969.

Cooling system

Centrifugal pump mounted in tandem with five-bladed fan and twin Vee-belt auxiliary drive. Twin thermostats. Capacity 28 pints (15.92 litres). Viscous coupled fan from 1968.

Below: The demonstration T-Type carrying the works number 1900 TU.

Petrol system

Twin independent electric pumps. Rear petrol tank capacity 23½ gallons (106.93 litres).

TRANSMISSION

Gearbox

Four-speed automatic (epicyclic with fluid coupling). From 1968, General Motors three-speed automatic with torque converter (400 type).

Ratios: 4-speed: Reverse, 4.30:1; First, 3.82:1; Second, 2.63:1; Third, 1.45:1; Fourth, direct

3-speed: Reverse, 2.08:1; First, 2.48:1; Second, 1.48:1; Third, direct.

Electrically operated gear selecter lever mounted on steering column. Torque converter multiplication at stall at 2.04:1.

Oil capacity: Four-speed 24 pints (13.65 litres).
Three-speed 18⅔ pints (10.613 litres).

Propeller shaft

Single-piece large-diameter tube with ball and trunnion front universal joint and needle roller universal joint at the rear.

Rear axle and final drive

Constant velocity inboard universal joints on axle half-shafts. Final drive unit carried on cross-member. Hypoid bevel final drive giving engine to road wheel ratio in top of 3.08:1.

Oil capacity 4½ pints (2.559 litres).

CHASSIS

Frame

Monocoque construction with front and rear sub-frames.

Suspension

Front independent with lower wishbone, upper stabilised lever, anti-roll bar and coil springs, (automatic hydraulic height control). Rear independent semi-trailing arms, anti-roll bar 1968, coil springs and (automatic hydraulic height control). 1969 height control, rear only. From August 1972, compliant front suspension.

Shock absorbers

Girling telescopic, front and rear; non-adjustable.

Brakes

High-pressure hydraulic with Girling (Rolls-Royce) 11in (279mm) front discs with two single-piston calipers. Rear discs with one dual-piston caliper. Three independent footbrake systems with servo power assistance from two engine-driven hydraulic pumps. Mechanical parking brake operated by right-hand acting on rear calipers only. Deceleration conscious pressure limiting valve on rear wheels. Ventilated front discs in 1973.

Steering

Power-assisted (Saginaw) rotary valve, integral ram steering box, low-friction recirculating ball. Later cars have collapsible steering column. Ratio: 1969, 19.3:1; 1971, 17.5:1.

Exhaust system

2in (50.8mm) bore exhaust system. Three silencers (part in stainless steel) i.e. silencer, expansion chamber, and resonator.

Wheels

6in x 15in (152mm x 381mm) pressed-steel disc wheels with five left- or right-hand threaded nuts.

Tyres

8.45in x 15in (215mm x 381mm) low profile by Dunlop. Avon or Firestone HR70 (235mm) HR15 low profile, tubeless (1974).

PRINCIPAL CHASSIS DETAILS AND DIMENSIONS

Wheelbase: Standard 9ft 11½in (3.035m); Long wheelbase 10ft 3½in (3.137m).

Track: Front and rear 4ft 9½in (1.461m).
Overall length: 16ft 11½in (5.169m).
Overall body width: 5ft 11in (1.803m).
Turning circle: 38ft 6in (11.735m).
Ground clearance: 6½in (165mm).
Weight: With standard body 40.70cwt (2,051.2kg).
 Increased weight 1976 42.4cwt (2,136.9kg).
Performance: Maximum speed 115mph (185.03km/h).
 Petrol consumption: 15mpg.
Price at introduction: £6,496 (including £924 purchase tax).
Number built: 1,692 (to 1976).

Note: Hydraulics; Two under-bonnet hydraulic accumulators maintained at 2,500psi, two under-bonnet reservoirs and two camshaft-driven piston pumps to operate hydraulic equipment.

Below: T-Type Corniche NBL 100L, chassis No DBH14439, engine No 14439, owned by Mr B.M. Russ-Turner of Surrey, England.

In 1971 the name Corniche was reborn, a two-door saloon and convertible being produced which was constructed on the universal base of the standard T-type saloon, by the coachbuilding subsidiary Mulliner Park Ward Ltd, at Willesden; the convertible being fitted with a power-operated hood.

This company had introduced a two-door saloon and convertible in 1966-7 and these models were replaced by the Corniche. The main shell was steel, with boot, doors and bonnet in aluminium alloy. It used a slightly deeper radiator than that of the standard T saloon, and was fitted with different and distinctive wheel trims. All the two-door cars were assembled in a special department, and coachwork and trimming were completed at the Hythe Road works of Mulliner Park Ward.

The engine was modified with twin Solex Carburettors and special air cleaner to give between five per cent and ten per cent more power; a 9.1 compression ratio, retimed camshaft, and revised air cleaner were some of the changes, and it was fitted with a six silencer, larger-bore twin-exhaust system.

The three-speed automatic gearbox with torque converter was the same as that used in the standard T saloon, as was the complete transmission line, including the electrically operated gearchange lever mounted on the steering column.

The car had a redesigned facia with the vital instrument grouped directly in front of the driver, and these included a tachometer and gauges for oil pressure and coolant.

Early cars had a 15in (381mm) wood-rimmed steering wheel, but later cars had the standard T-type plastic-covered 16in (406.4mm) wheel. Automatic speed control became standard late in 1973.

The car was largely hand-built, and each one was given fourteen to twenty coats of paint and took at least four months to build. Any colour could be specified by the customer.

In April 1974, *Autocar* road-tested a two-door saloon (in Rolls-Royce form), and it reached a maximum (best) speed of 122mph (196.298km/h) at about 4,750 revolutions a minute. Acceleration tests gave figures of 0 to 60mph (96.54km/h) in 9.6 seconds, and 0 to 100mph (160.9km/h) in 30 seconds, some of these being achieved with impressive wheel-spin!

Recent production cars no longer have any distinguishable mechanical features from the standard T-type saloon, and the differences are purely cosmetic.

However, the glamour of the name continues, and a Bentley Corniche still conjures up visions of smooth, swift motoring, in a car which retains its distinctive character and which gives the driver such immense pleasure.

SPECIFICATION

T-TYPE CORNICHE

In production 1971-77.

Basic specification at introduction as for T-Type except as follows:

ENGINE

Bore	4.1in (104.1mm)
Stroke	3.9in (99.1mm)
Cubic capacity	6,750cc (411.9 cu in)
Compression ratio	9.0:1; 1975, 8.0:1
Brake horsepower	not disclosed

Generator
As T-Type but with tachometer, automatic speed control.

Instruments
As T-Type but with tachometer automatic speed control.

Cooling system
Centrifugal pump and thermostat. Five-assymetric-bladed fan with viscous drive. Capacity 28½ pints (16.209 litres). Full air-conditioning.

TRANSMISSION
Gearbox
Three-speed and torque converter as T-Type with anti-theft device in selector circuit.

CHASSIS
Exhaust system
Six silencers on twin exhaust system 2¼in (57mm) bore pipes. Last two boxes and pipes of stainless steel.

PRINCIPAL CHASSIS DETAILS AND DIMENSIONS
(Two-door Saloon)
Wheelbase: 9ft 11½in (3.035m).
Track: 4ft 11½in (1.511m).
Overall length: 16ft 11½in (5.169m).
Overall body width: 6ft 0½in (1.841m).
Turning circle: Right 40ft 2in (12.243m), Left 40ft 11in (12.471m)
Ground clearance: 6½in (165mm).
Weight: 41¾cwt (2,104kg).
Performance: Maximum speed 120mph (193.08km/h).
 Petrol consumption 15mpg.
Price at introduction: £12,758 (including £2,988 purchase tax for two-door saloon).
Number built: 221 (to 1976).

T2-Type

Early in 1977, rumours of a new Bentley were spreading in motoring circles and in February 1977 *Autocar* and *Motor* both carried reports on the re-vamped car which was announced.

The general feeling expressed was that the factory design team had worked wonders on the car in respect of handling and steering. New rack and pinion gear had vastly improved the 'feel' and given a more precise control, especially when driven enthusiastically, although power assistance was still retained. The modified front suspension had raised upper suspension arm joints enabling the wheels to retain a more vertical movement when cornering, in addition body roll was reduced and tyre life increased; a smaller 15¼in (387mm) diameter steering wheel was utilised.

A few further changes were made to the 6,750cc (411.9cu in) engine, but new type SU carburettors were now fitted with a smaller choke but a small loss of top-end power was adequately made up by fitting the twin-pipe exhaust system, previously used by the Corniche. The overall effect was improved middle-range torque and better fuel consumption. The instrument panel was entirely new and incorporated in the fascia were the controls for the split-level air-conditioning system and a new electronic speed-

ometer, removing the last cable from the control and reporting systems, together with fuel level, oil pressure, ammeter and water temperature gauges (almost a return to vintage practice!), and at last a mileage recorder trip reset was fitted. The fascia panel also had an ambient air temperature gauge and carried the Econocruise electronic speed controls.

The appearance of the car was only slightly changed, more so at the front, where an airdam has been built-in under the front bumper, albeit termed an 'anti-lift' panel, the effect of which is to improve straight-line stability.

The changes otherwise were the adoption of American-style shock absorber type bumpers, in a retracted position, consisting of a steel beam with polyurethane inserts. The radiator shell was about .047in deeper, a pleasant return to boldness, and there were small specification changes with regard to the door handles and

Below and facing page: Type T2 saloon TUE 434R, chassis No SBH31457, engine No 31457, registered June 1977, the property of Mr R.A. Parker of Warwickshire, England.

the under-bumper-fitted fog lights.

Some two hundred changes have been made to the T-Type since its arrival on the motoring scene in 1965, all part of the factory policy of continuous development, resulting in a superb car surely entitled to be called the finest in the world.

SPECIFICATION

T2-TYPE

In production from 1977.

Basic specification at introduction as for T-Type except as follows:

ENGINE
Lubrication
Throw-away filter canister.

Carburettors
Twin SU HIF7s with temperature compensation (Note: IF = integral float chamber).

Generator
75 amp alternator.

Instruments
New facia, electronic speedometer and ambient air temperature gauge.

Cooling system
Viscous coupled seven-bladed fan plus electric fan in front of radiator.

CHASSIS
Suspension
Altered geometry of front suspension and reduced diameter rear anti-roll bar.

Steering
Burman rack and pinion.

Exhaust system
Twin exhaust system with six silencer boxes (three each side), the rear boxes and tailpipe in stainless steel, centre boxes nickel-plated and first boxes mild steel.

PRINCIPAL CHASSIS DETAILS AND DIMENSIONS
Wheelbase: 10ft (3.048m).
Track: Front 5ft (1.524m); Rear 4ft 11½in (1.511m).
Overall length: 17ft (5.182m).
Overall body width: 5ft 11¾in (1.822m).
Ground clearance: 6½in (165mm).
Weight: With standard body 44cwt (2,217.5kg).
Performance: Maximum speed 118mph (188km/h).
Petrol consumption 14-15mpg.
Price at introduction: £22,809.15 (including £1,624.58 car tax, £1,689.57 VAT).

A Full Circle

After the end of the Second World War, the aero-engine activities of Rolls-Royce Ltd, the parent Company, expanded very considerably with the development of gas turbine engines; they were further enlarged in 1966 by the acquisition of Bristol Siddeley Engines Ltd.

In 1971 serious financial difficulties attributable to the RB211 project led the Board of Rolls-Royce to request Royal Exchange Insurance to appoint a receiver for the debenture stockholders and on 4 February 1971 Mr E.R. Nicholson was appointed receiver and manager of Rolls-Royce and of H.J. Mulliner, Park Ward. Shortly after, the Government incorporated a new company to purchase all four divisions concerned with gas turbine engines and named it Rolls-Royce (1971) Ltd. Rolls-Royce Ltd was placed in liquidation on the 4 October 1971, which included its subsidiary Bentley Motors (1931) Ltd.

Rolls-Royce Motors Ltd, a wholly owned subsidiary of Rolls-Royce (1971) Ltd, commenced trading in April 1971, as agent for the receiver of Rolls-Royce Ltd and H.J. Mulliner, Park Ward Ltd.

On 19 June 1971 Rolls-Royce Motors Holdings Ltd was formed, taking over the Car Manufacturing Division.

Late 1971 saw the closing of another chapter in the history of the Bentley Motor Car, when W.O. Bentley, MBE, and holder of the Merite Sportif Français (awarded to him in 1969 by the French Minister of Sport), died on the 14 August, aged 83. It would perhaps have been interesting to know his feelings on the financial problems that were besetting the company that owned the Bentley name. Recollections of the problems he faced on 17 December 1931, when Bentley Motors (1931) Ltd was formed, might have been accompanied by a wry smile.

The final restructuring operations resulted in the name of the subsidiary being changed to Bentley Motors Ltd, with effect from 24 September 1973; the wheel had turned full circle.

One of the first and one of the newest – the 3-litre of 1921 and the T2 of 1977.

Bentleys in Action

Pictures at Silverstone:

Left: Bentley Drivers Club stalwart, the late Harry Rose in the Paddock waiting to go on to the starting grid in 1968.

Below: John Goddard at Silverstone in his turbo-charged 3/8-litre Bentley. The fastest Bentley in the world 158.2mph (254.54km/h) for the flying kilometre on the Kennedylaan Highway near Ghent, Belgium, in May 1972.

Top right: Barry Eastick's 6¼-litre T-Type special on the grid, 1977.

Bottom right: Vintage line up waiting for the starter, 1977.

Credits

J. Alexander: 71 (Bottom right)

Douglas Allen: 68 (Top)

Autocar: 14/15, 96/97, 107 (Top), 123 (Top), 136 (Lower), 180, 188, 198/199, 210

Aviemore Photographic: 34 (Top)

Bentley Drivers Club: 31

Chas K. Bowers: 106, 110, 132

T. P. Breen: 62 (Top, Middle and Lower)

M. Collier: 187, 201

Red Daniels: 7, 33 (Top right)

A. Dumage: 36 (Top right)

M. B. Gaudin: 57 (Top left)

H. N. Harben: 60 (Top left)

N. Hood: 36 (Top left)

C. Lang: 168, 169

D. Llewelyn: 35

R. E. May: 71 (Upper and Lower centre left)

D. Miller-Williams: 34 (Lower)

Roy Norton: 186

Ivo Peters: 65 (Middle)

R. S. Pulvertaft: 196

R. V. Roberts: 10, 28 (Centre), 91 (Top)

Rolls-Royce Ltd: 11, 13, 44, 45, 46, 47, 48, 49, 72, 74, 75, 106, 122, 123 (Lower), 134, 136 (Top and Middle), 142 (Top), 156, 157 (Bottom), 159, 160 (Top), 182, 183 (Middle and Bottom), 189, 190, 204, 206, 207, 211, 214, 216

C. B. D. Sargent: 138, 139

Science Museum, London: 147 (Middle and Lower)

S. Sedgwick: 178, 179, 200

J. Smith: 33 (Top left)

R. P. Stowers: 140, 105, 198

G. L. Steward: 160 (Middle and Bottom), 161

J. J. Stickley: 64, 65 (Top left and right), 65 (Bottom)

N. W. Stickney: 157 (Top)

G. Tabbenor: 51 (Middle left)

T. J. Threlfall: 51 (Middle right)

R. D. Weary: 111

A. Wood: 181

All other photographs by John Adams, AIIP

Bentley and Rolls-Royce badges and trademarks are reproduced by permission of Rolls-Royce Motors Limited

One of the supercharged 4½-litres once owned by the Hon Dorothy Paget: YU 3250 (featured on pages 102 and 103) on the grid at Silverstone in 1976 with Harvey Hine at the wheel.